# PSEUDO-PLATO, *AXIOCHUS*

Society of Biblical Literature

## TEXTS AND TRANSLATIONS
## GRAECO-ROMAN RELIGION SERIES

edited by
Hans Dieter Betz
Edward N. O'Neil

Texts and Translations 21
Graeco-Roman Religion Series 6

# PSEUDO-PLATO,
# *AXIOCHUS*

by
Jackson P. Hershbell

# PSEUDO-PLATO, *AXIOCHUS*

by Jackson P. Hershbell

Scholars Press

Distributed by
Scholars Press
101 Salem Street
Chico, California 95926

# PSEUDO-PLATO, *AXIOCHUS*

by

## Jackson P. Hershbell

**Library of Congress Cataloging in Publication Data**

Hershbell, Jackson P    1935–
    Pseudo-Plato, Axiochus.

    (Graeco-Roman religion series ; 6 ISSN 0145-3211)
(Texts and translations ; 21 ISSN 0145-3203)
        Bibliography: p.
        Includes indexes.
        1. Plato. Spurious and doubtful works. Axiochus.
2. Death–Early works to 1800. I. Plato. Spurious
and doubtful works. Axiochus. English. 1980.
II. Title. III. Series. IV. Series: Society of
Biblical Literature. Texts and translations ; 21.
B391. A85H47        128'.5        79-20127
ISBN 0-89130-354-5 pbk.

Printed in the United States of America
1 2 3 4 5 6
Edwards Brothers, Inc.
Ann Arbor, Michigan 48104

# TABLE OF CONTENTS

PREFACE . . . . . . . . . . . . . . . . . . . . . .  vii

INTRODUCTION . . . . . . . . . . . . . . . . . . . .  1

   I. The Dialogue and the Understanding of
     Greek Religion and Philosophy . . . . . . .  1

  II. The Structure of the Work . . . . . . . . . .  8

 III. The Origin of the Work . . . . . . . . . . . .  10

     A. Linguistic Evidence . . . . . . . . . . . .  12

     B. Historical Evidence . . . . . . . . . . . .  13

     C. Philosophical Evidence . . . . . . . . . .  14

  IV. Literary Genre . . . . . . . . . . . . . . . .  19

   V. Date and Authorship of the *Axiochus* . . . . .  20

NOTES TO PREFACE AND INTRODUCTION . . . . . . . . . .  23

TEXT AND TRANSLATION . . . . . . . . . . . . . . . .  27

NOTES TO TRANSLATION . . . . . . . . . . . . . . . .  53

SELECT BIBLIOGRAPHY . . . . . . . . . . . . . . . .  71

INDEX I: NAMES, ANCIENT AND MODERN . . . . . . . . .  75

INDEX II: ANCIENT PASSAGES . . . . . . . . . . . . .  79

INDEX III: GREEK TERMS . . . . . . . . . . . . . . .  87

# PREFACE

Until the present, only three English translations of the *Axiochus* have appeared: one attributed to Edmund Spenser, a "lost work" of his, first published in 1592, and in facsimile in 1934; an English translation in 1607 of Philippe de Mornay's French version of 1581; and that of E. H. Blakeney in 1937.[1] Spenser's interest in the work is no surprise since it was a favorite in the Renaissance, and prior to 1592 had been translated many times into French, Italian, Latin, and Spanish.[2] By most scholars then, the *Axiochus* was attributed to Plato, although its authenticity was being questioned. Marsilio Ficino, for example, as early as 1477, assigned the dialogue to Xenocrates.[3] But until the nineteenth century, there seems to have been little extensive or serious scholarship on the work, especially in English. Even Blakeney's "little book" of 1937 was undertaken "not for the learned but for learners,"[4] providing with its notes a useful but general introduction to the dialogue. Blakeney failed, however, to consult studies not in English, e.g. those of Chevalier, Feddersen, Immisch, Souilhé, and he showed little understanding of the problems posed by the dialogue.

The following introduction, text, translation, and commentary have been undertaken with the hope of bringing the *Axiochus* into focus with previous scholarship and helping the reader to understand the difficulties of this small work. Standard abbreviations of ancient authors are given in accordance with Liddell and Scott, *Greek-English Lexicon* (*LSJ*); Bauer, *A Greek-English Lexicon of the New Testament and other Early Christian Literature*; and Lewis and Short, *A Latin Dictionary*. The text used is that of J. Souilhé, which is basically the same as that of J. Burnet, but with a more extensive critical apparatus.

Indices of ancient and modern names, ancient passages, and Greek terms were composed by Professor Edward O'Neil.

vii

Special thanks are due to Hans Dieter Betz, Roy Kotansky, and Professor O'Neil. I am especially indebted to Professor Betz for making useful criticisms on the introduction and commentary, and to Professor O'Neil for his critique of my translation, as well as for the indices. Both colleagues saved me from many errors and oversights. Whatever faults remain are entirely my own.

Since much of the preliminary work was done at the University of Munich, I would like to thank the Alexander von Humboldt-Stiftung for making possible a year of study from the fall of 1977 to that of 1978.


Jackson P. Hershbell
Minneapolis, Minnesota

April 1981

INTRODUCTION

I.  The Dialogue and the Understanding of Greek Religion
    and Philosophy

Scholars have often criticized the *Axiochus* for its
lack of originality and consistency, but the work should
not be measured by these standards.[5] It can more properly
be viewed as a good summary of Greek religious-philosophical
thought about death as probably held in the second or first
century B.C., thus as an important example of the syncretism which became common in late antiquity, before and dur-
ing the advent of Christianity.  In particular, it is a
curious blending of Epicurean and Platonic views on the
soul and afterlife.  Cynic and Stoic influences are also
discernible in the dialogue, and it may also, as many
scholars have thought, reflect Orphic and Pythagorean
beliefs.

Without doubt, the *Axiochus* is one of numerous works,
known as "consolations," composed in antiquity under the
initial inspiration of Plato's *Phaedo*.  The Platonic influence on the *Axiochus* is manifest not only in the Athenian
setting and personae of the dialogue, especially the figure
of Socrates, but also in some of its main conceptions such
as the immortality of the soul with the concomitant belief
that the body is a prison or tomb for the soul (*Ax.* 366A,
370D; cf. *Phd.* 62B, 82F and *Grg.* 493A); when the soul is
released from the body, it will lead a fairer and purer
kind of life (*Ax.* 370C-D; cf. *Phd.* 114B-C).  Also the myth
which concludes the *Axiochus* (371A-372), with its description
of the soul's wanderings after death, the judgment of Minos
and Rhadamanthys, the fates of the wicked and virtuous, has
probably been modeled, in part, after the eschatological
myths of Plato's *Phaedo*, *Gorgias*, and *Republic* (Bk. 10).
Much of this material, however, is also Orphic-Pythagorean.
Certainly the body-tomb (*sōma-sēma*) doctrine is found in

1

Orphism, and both Orphics and Pythagoreans believed in the soul's immortality.[6] Their influence on Plato has often been claimed,[7] and thus, although he remains the main authority for the author of the *Axiochus*, Orphic-Pythagorean elements in the dialogue cannot be easily dismissed.

But in addition to teachings of Plato, the *Axiochus* also contains doctrines of Epicurus, all of which may be considered variations on the theme that "death is nothing to us" (*Sent.* 2, apud D. L. 10.139). For as a lapse into total and permanent unconsciousness, death concerns neither the living--for they are--nor the dead--for they no longer are (369C). Death is thus not to be feared, and is, in fact, a release from the ills and pains of this life. *Axiochus* rejects, however, the view of death as complete annihilation as "the current chatter of the times" (369D), and Immisch may be right in concluding that the *Axiochus* is an anti-Epicurean polemic, intended to contrast Platonic with Epicurean answers to the perennial problem of what may be hoped for after life.[8]

Since the *Axiochus* seems intended for a popular audience, however, no mention is made in it of the basic metaphysical premises on which these competing views of death were based: for the Epicureans, atoms and the void, and for the Platonists, the world of Ideas or Forms. On the whole, it appears that the author of the *Axiochus* was not very interested in complicated or sophisticated philosophical theories. Without discussion of their original theoretical frameworks, he took two by then popular but incompatible views of death and fashioned his consolation in such a way that belief in an afterlife prevails over that in total extinction. Certainly the dialogue's concluding myth confirms the author's interest in maintaining the soul's immortality, and with it the importance of leading a good (moral) life in this world. Diverse as the sources of the myth may be, it is well within the tradition of Platonic eschatological myths, both Plato's own and those of later Platonists such as Plutarch, e.g. his *De genio Socr.* 590-592F or *De sera num. vind.* 563B-568. Like these myths, that of the *Axiochus* stresses the view that whether above or below (ἥ κάτω ἥ ἄνω), you must be in a state of well-being if you have lived piously (εὐδαιμονεῖν σε δεῖ...βεβιωκότα εὐσεβῶς, 372).

The immortality of the soul expounded by Socrates in the latter part of the *Axiochus* is, however, not strictly an ethical or philosophical notion. It is also bound up with religious beliefs. According to Socrates, the soul's immortality is proved by human achievements in the ascent from brutish existence to civilization, especially by the creation of astronomy, the science which reveals the *magnalia Dei*. For humanity could not have done these things unless there were a "divine spirit in the soul" by which we have so much intelligence and knowledge (370C). Common as this idea of an immanent divine spirit was among authors of the Greco-Roman period, e.g. Posidonius, Cicero, Seneca, Plutarch, it is given concise treatment in connection with the soul's immortality in the *Axiochus*.[9]

The concluding myth of the *Axiochus*, with its description of the underworld, also offers a wealth of material for a student of ancient Greek religion. The sources for the myth are no doubt many and varied. For example, the depiction of the life of the pious in the underworld can be traced back to the Homeric poems, e.g. *Odyssey* 4.563-69 with its brief description of the Elysian Plain, or to Pindar (*Frag.* 129 and 130, ed. Christ, quoted in Plutarch *Cons. ad Apoll.* 120C, cf. *Ax.* 371C-E).

> On them is lit the strength of the sun beneath
>     the darkness we know here,
> and the space before the city of them lies in
>     bright-flowering meadows,
> shadowy with incense-trees and heavy with golden
>     fruits.
> And some with horses and exercise, some with
>     draught-games,
> some with lyres take their pleasure, and a whole
>     life of bliss breaks into flower upon them.

A lovely fragrance is scattered across the place
as they join all manner of sacrifices to bright
    fire on the gods' altars. (R. Lattimore's trans.)

Still other elements of the *Axiochus* myth can be found
in Greek literature. The punishment of the wicked, especially Tityus, Tantalus, and Sisyphus, can be traced back
to *Odyssey* 11.575-600. And notions similar to the "well
arranged drinking parties and self-furnished banquets"
(συμπόσιά τε εὐμελῆ καὶ εἰλαπίναι αὐτοχορηγήται, 371D) appear in Plutarch (*De sera num. vind.* 565F) and in Lucian
(*VH* 2.5 and 14), where the blessed enjoy feasts and drinking in the afterlife. Perhaps the ultimate source for this
conception is Orphic, for Plato writes in the *Republic*:[10]

> And Musaeus and his son have a more excellent song
> than these of the blessings that the gods bestow
> on the righteous. For they conduct them to the
> house of Hades in their tale and arrange a sympos-
> ium of the saints, where, reclined on couches and
> crowned with wreaths, they entertain the time
> henceforth with wine, as if the fairest meed of
> virtue were an everlasting drunk. (363C)

Also important for understanding the *Axiochus* myth are
its allusions to the Eleusinian mysteries. In the afterlife, there is a "place of honor for those who are initiated" (τοῖς μεμυημένοις ἐστί τις προεδρία), and before beginning their descent to Hades, Dionysus and Heracles were
initiated and encouraged by the goddess of Eleusis
(371D-E).[11] Now one of the essential features of the
Eleusinian mysteries was the confidence they gave to the
initiates for the hereafter, not so much because their
souls would survive, but because of the kind of survival
promised: the souls of the initiated would have a blessed
existence, those of the uninitiated a miserable one. Thus
Isocrates (*Paneg.* 28) writes that one of the benefits of
the mysteries was that those who shared in its rites "had
sweeter expectations for all eternity" (...τοῦ σύμπαντος
αἰῶνος ἡδίους τὰς ἐλπίδας ἔχουσι); cf. the *Homeric Hymn to
Demeter*, 480-82: "happy is he among men upon earth who has

seen these mysteries; but he who is uninitiate...never has
lot of like good things once he is dead, down in darkness
and gloom." In Diogenes Laertius' life of Diogenes of
Sinope (6.39), it is reported that the Athenians urged him
to be initiated, for those in the other world would obtain
a special place of honor (...ἐν ᾅδου προεδρίας οἱ μεμυημένοι τυγχάνουσι. And the connections of Dionysus and Heracles with the Eleusinian mysteries are known from both
literary sources and vase-paintings.[12]

In sum, the *Axiochus*, especially its myth, contains an
unusual synthesis of religious beliefs of the ancient world,
many of which can be traced back to Homer, Pindar, Plato,
the Orphic-Pythagorean tradition, and to the Eleusinian
mysteries. And Nilsson is probably right in remarking that
the myth shows that "old ideas about the underworld have
not lost their force."[13]

Besides the traditional or popular Greek religious
conceptions of the *Axiochus*, some mention should be made of
the dialogue's occasional similarities to early Christian
thought. Chevalier noted that the earliest reference to
the work is in Diogenes Laertius (ca. second-third century
A.D.), and that several expressions or beliefs are curious-
ly like those found in early Christian literature.[14] Among
the more striking cited by Chevalier are: (1) the term
σκῆνος (366A) applied to the human body--it appears already
in Democritus (e.g. B37 and B187), and then rather frequent-
ly in the early Christian period: in 2 Cor 5:4 (cf. σκήνωμα
in 2 Pet 1:13f.); *Dg.* 6:8; *Corp. Herm.* XIII.12,15; *Papyri
Graecae Magicae*; Ach. Tat. II.36.3; and the LXX. (2) γέγονα
καινός (370E)--"I have become a new man"; this sense of
καινός seems unknown to the pre-Christian world. Plutarch
used the expression (*Cat. Ma.* 1), but to refer to a *homo
novus* in a social context; only in the NT is it found in
the sense of "renewed within" (on καινός, 2 Cor 5:17, Gal
6:15, Eph 4:24; on καινότης, Rom 6:4, ἐν καινότητι πνεύμα-
τος (cf. Rom 7:6). (3) εἰ μή τι Θεῖον ὄντως ἐνῆν πνεῦμα

τῇ ψυχῇ (370C), where *pneuma* is used to designate neither
the soul itself, nor a superior part of the soul (as used
by Xenocrates and the Stoics), but something divine in us,
indeed the effect of divine action on the soul.  A similar
idea is found in early Christian thought, e.g. Paul's conviction that the Christian has the divine *pneuma* and is
thus different from others  leads  him to use this word to
characterize the believer's inner being, e.g. Rom 8:16,
"the spirit itself (of God) witnesses together with our
spirit..." (αὐτὸ τὸ πνεῦμα συμμαρτυρεῖ τῷ πνεύματι ἡμῶν...);
and in 1 Thess 5:23 and Heb 4:12, a distinction similar to
that of the *Axiochus* between soul (*psychē*) and spirit
(*pneuma*) is made.  Although Chevalier himself considered
these and other resemblances between the *Axiochus* and early
Christian writings more exterior than profound, they nonetheless suggest some affinity between the texts, an affinity
arising probably from the mystery cults and from related
"philosophical" and "religious" language.[15]

The *Axiochus* has, despite sometimes negative assess-
ments, continued throughout the centuries to attract attention.  It was especially valued by Byzantine scholars such
as Stobaeus who in his Περὶ τοῦ βίου (98, 75. Mein. III.
236: cf. *Ax*. 366 f.), ῎Επαινος θανάτου (120, 34-35. Mein.
IV. 121: cf. *Ax*. 365B, 369B), and Σύγκρισις ζωῆς καὶ θανάτου (121, 38. Mein. IV. 121; cf. *Ax*. 365E), quoted long
passages from it.  In the twelfth century, Theodorus Prodromus or Hilarion also spoke of the dialogue with praise.
But it was in the Renaissance that the *Axiochus* was read,
translated, and commented on with great enthusiasm.  The
reasons for this phenomenon have been briefly but well
explained by Chevalier, who observed that the Renaissance
humanists' desire for form and their love of rhetoric were
well satisfied by the *Axiochus*.  Some, such as Marsilio
Ficino, also saw in the dialogue an anticipation of Christianity and the moral life.[16]

In the sixteenth century, however, doubts about the
value of the *Axiochus* began to be raised, and Montaigne,
for example, wrote in his *Essais*:

> When I find myself disliking Plato's *Axiochus*, as
> a work without power considering who the author
> was, my judgment does not trust itself; it is not
> so foolish as to oppose itself to the authority
> of so many other famous judgments of antiquity,
> which it considers as its mentors and masters and
> with whom it is rather content to err. It blames
> and condemns itself either for stopping at the
> outer bark, not being able to penetrate to the
> heart, or for looking at it by some false light.
> It is content with only securing itself from con-
> fusion and disorder; as to its own weakness, it
> frankly acknowledges and confesses it. It thinks
> it gives a just interpretation to the appearances
> that its apprehension presents to it; but they
> are weak and imperfect. (*Of Books*, trans. C.
> Cotton-W. Hazlitt)

Although Montaigne's opinion was generally accepted, subsequent judgments on the *Axiochus* have varied. Scholars such
as Fabricius, Boeckh, Welcker, considered it in a favorable
light, Fabricius remarking, for example,

> whatever the case may be, the author is most
> ancient and eloquent, and the dialogue, as Fischer
> believes, is excellent among its kind and elegantly
> composed, so that the vestiges of its ancient re-
> finement and teaching as well as its Greek eloquence
> are everywhere clearly discerned.

But later in the nineteenth and early twentieth centuries,
scholars such as Susemihl, Heinze, Rohde, Immisch, Wilamowitz, all shared something of Meiners' opinion who believed
that a "work of this kind could have only been written by a
barbarian or semi-barbarian."[17]

In historical retrospect, the *Axiochus* cannot be ex-
cessively admired or condemned. Each age has its own literary tastes, and despite negative judgments such as that
of Meiners, the *Axiochus* remains, with its oddities and
peculiar charm, an interesting and important document stem-
ming probably from the age of anxiety in which Christianity

made its appearance. Platonic, Epicurean, Stoic, Cynic, and other philosophical and religious beliefs were then in circulation, all competing to offer solutions to life's difficulties. Yet, however satisfactory their solutions may have been, death remained for Axiochus and his contemporaries a problem. So it remains for us today, and a twentieth-century consolation would probably not offer better alternatives than those of Socrates. The *Axiochus'* attempt to deal with death may sometimes seem awkward or even amusing, but its subject remains a perennial and perplexing one.

II. The Structure of the Work

At the beginning of the *Axiochus*, Socrates narrates a past event in which he has been both observer and participant. Then, with an almost imperceptible transition from narrative to dramatic form, the work continues as if several persons were present, presumably Cleinias, Damon, and Charmides, but the last two say nothing. Even Cleinias, who summons Socrates to his father's bed, becomes a silent onlooker. The main part of the dialogue consists of exchanges between Socrates and Axiochus, the latter mostly reacting to Socrates' arguments which try to show that one should not fear death, but rather desire it. A reasonable division of the dialogue, in accord with those made by Chevalier and Souilhé,[18] is as follows.

Part I:

A. *Introduction* (364-365A): summoned by Cleinias, Socrates goes to the dying Axiochus and attempts to console him.

B. *The Initial Consolation* (365A-B): Socrates attempts to persuade Axiochus to accept his fate without complaint, and to realize that life is only a sojourn in a foreign land. Several "proofs" follow in which Socrates tries to show Axiochus that it is not necessary to fear the loss of life and its benefits.

1. *First Argument* (365D-366B): Axiochus laments
   his impending loss of consciousness with his
   awareness of joys and pleasures, and fears
   the decay of his body. But, replies Socrates,
   is his attitude not inconsistent? For if
   Axiochus will lapse into complete insensibility, what evil can befall him? Since we are
   a soul, the destruction of the body-soul
   composite can only herald a transition to a
   better state in which Axiochus is freed from
   bodily miseries.

2. *Second Argument* (366D-369B): Socrates recalls
   a lecture of Prodicus in which the Sophist
   presented the miseries of life's changes.
   From infancy to old age, life is full of pain,
   and the gods quickly release those whom they
   love. There is thus no reason to cling pas-
   sionately to life.

3. *Third Argument* (369B-D): Socrates also borrows
   this argument from Prodicus: death can neither
   affect the living because they exist, nor the
   dead since they no longer are and thus cannot
   be troubled. Axiochus replies that these are
   sophistic arguments, the fashionable talk of
   the times, and do not provide genuine consolation (369D).

Part II:

Socrates abandons his previous arguments, and
attempts to demonstrate the soul's well-being
after death.

4. *Fourth Argument* (370B-371): Socrates believes
   the soul's immortality is revealed by the
   great undertakings of the human race, e.g.
   the conquest of nature, the establishment of
   cities and governments, especially the con-
   templation and study of the heavens. Unless
   a divine spirit (*pneuma*) were really present
   in the soul, mankind could not know and understand the workings of the universe. When the
   soul is finally released from its prison, the
   body, Axiochus will experience a life of joy
   and peace.

Axiochus confesses that he no longer fears death,
but longs for it: "I have become a new person."

*Confirmation by a Myth* (371A-end): The discourse
of Gobryas supports some of Socrates' preceding
remarks. So Socrates reports what Gobryas, a Persian wise man, has learned from bronze tablets on
Delos: the souls of the just or righteous have a

life of joy and true pleasure; those of the unjust
or corrupt pay for their misdeeds in a life of
eternal torment.  Socrates, however, will not affirm
the truth of the myth's details, even though he is
convinced that all souls are immortal and that when
removed from this corporeal existence, they will
have unending bliss if they have lived piously.

Axiochus is now fully persuaded about the soul's immortality, and the consolation is complete: no longer does
he fear death, but rather desires it.

III.  The Origin of the Work

Neglect of the *Axiochus* among nonspecialists is perhaps understandable.  Certainly its style, "adorned with
poetic words, odd expressions, bizarre turns of phrasing,"
seems unworthy of Plato, not to mention various philosophical inconsistencies, and anachronisms.[19]  Twentieth-century
criticism, supported by Diogenes Laertius (3.62), who lists
the dialogue among those acknowledged to be spurious
(νοθεύονται...ὁμολογουμένως), is unanimous in considering
the work pseudo-Platonic.  The reasons for rejecting Plato's
authorship are numerous, but P. Shorey succinctly summarized
them by remarking:[20]

> The spuriousness of the *Axiochus* is sufficiently
> proved by its vocabulary and its use of commonplace
> Stoic and Epicurean topics of the post-Platonic
> literature of consolations.

But if the dialogue is not by Plato, who was its author,
and when was it written?  For what reasons?  Answers to
these questions are hardly unanimous.

At 2.61 of his *Lives and Opinions of Eminent Philosophers*, for example, Diogenes Laertius attributed an *Axiochus*
to Aeschines, a disciple of Socrates, and on the basis of
this report, some scholars, notably Buresch, argued for
Aeschines' authorship of the present dialogue.  His views,
however, have not found acceptance, and evidence against
Aeschines' authorship is considerable.  First, the ancients

regarded Aeschines' dialogues as models of Attic prose, and
they were known to be long and sophisticated (ὁ τοὺς
μακροὺς καὶ ἀστείους διαλόγους γράψας, Lucian, *Par.* 32),
properties hardly attributable to the present *Axiochus*.
Second, aside from style, if the work is by Aeschines, how
are allusions or references to Epicurus' doctrines explained?  Buresch claimed that the fragments of Epicurus
are citations or imitations of the *Axiochus*, but as Chevalier showed, the reverse seems to be the case.[21]

On the whole, a brief survey of previous opinions
about the dialogue's authorship shows how uncertain conclu-
sions on this matter are.  Marsilio Ficino, for example,
attributed it to Xenocrates, noting that Diogenes Laertius
listed a Περὶ θανάτου ά among the latter's works (4.12).
Yet the name of Xenocrates appears on no manuscript of the
*Axiochus*, and he apparently did not compose dialogues but
rather treatises in the manner of Aristotle.  Meister
thought that the style and content were derived from Posidonius.  Taylor and Immisch believed the dialogue was composed by a member of the Academy against Epicurus near the
end of the fourth century B.C.  Chevalier found the work's
language late, and written under neo-Pythagorean influence
not before the first century B.C., an opinion shared to
some extent by Souilhé.  Blakeney, accepting some of Taylor's views, thought it unnecessary to assign the *Axiochus*
composition to "so late a date as the first century B.C."[22]

The previous survey of scholarly opinion strongly suggests that the question of specific authorship is unanswer-
able.  Reasons for not assigning the work to Plato (aside
from Diogenes Laertius' report), however, seem decisive.
Evidence for non-Platonic and probably late authorship is
basically of three kinds: linguistic, historical, and philosophical.  To be sure, these categories are not mutually
exclusive.  For example, a term not documented before the
second century B.C. may be "historical evidence" for late

composition, but in itself is not final proof. The categories must be taken in conjunction, and they are introduced only for easier comprehension of an often complex and
extensive collection of data.

A.  Linguistic Evidence

The language of the *Axiochus*, especially vocabulary
and syntax, was extensively studied by Chevalier, and on
the basis of his research it seems clear that the dialogue
belongs neither to the fourth nor to the third century
B.C.[23] Neologisms or terms apparently unknown to Plato
abound, and Chevalier lists a number found in the opening
sections of the work: 364B, αἰφνιδίου, διαχλευάζων; 364C,
ἐπιτωθάζων, παρηγόρησον, ἀστενακτί, ἐς τὸ χρεὼν ἴη, ἀτυχήσεις μου; 364D, ἀνασφῆλαι; 365A, the plural τὰς ἀφάς,
ῥωμαλέον.

Some of these and other terms are found only in later
authors, e.g.: ἐπιτωθάζων (364C, and App., *BC* 2.67 and
5.125; Ath. XIII.604E; Philostr., *VS* 38.21); παρεπιδημία
(365B and e.g. Polybius, 4.4,2, etc.; Plutarch *Tim*. 38,
*Eum*. 1; Ath. V.196A; XII.538C; XIII.579A; Ael., *VH* 90.29
[Hercher]); the prose usage of πληθύς (366B and not before
Plutarch and Lucian); δίμοιρον (366C and only in Plutarch,
*C.G.* 17); and συνερανίζω (369A and also in Plutarch, *De
sollert. an.* 963B). Other terms appear quite often in
later writers, e.g.: ῥωμαλέος (365A and in Galen, Aristides
Rhetor, Aelian); πρὸς κακοῦ (366A and Philodemus, Galen,
Clement of Alexandria); κριτικός (366E and Polybius 32.
4,5; Galen, Aristides Rhetor [*Or*. XII.136 Dindorf]), and
ἀψίκορος (369A and Polybius, Plutarch, and Lucian). A number of hapax legomena also appear in the dialogue, e.g.
ἀμυχαῖος (366A), ἀπηχήματα (366C), περιψυγμόν (366D), and
αὐτοχορήγητος (371D). To be sure, hapax legomena as such
do not prove late authorship, but taken together with the
previous linguistic data and the fact that the *Axiochus*
abounds in strange terms, expressions, and constructions,

sometimes "hardly Greek" and "for the most part, of a late
date," Chevalier and others seem justified in assigning it
to a period later than Plato.[24]

B.  Historical Evidence

The historical material is also important for dating
the work.  Although the author refers to Socrates' Athens
from the dialogue's very beginning, e.g. the Cynosarges,
Ilisus, Callirrhoe (364A ff.), the battle of Arginusae
(368D-F), or the discourse of Prodicus (366E-367A), anachronisms exist.  The section, for example, dealing with
the education of young boys and ephebes (366D-367B) has
aroused much suspicion about Platonic or fourth-century
authorship.  No text, except the *Axiochus*, mentions the
παιδοτρίβης ("physical trainer") among the instructors of
young boys, circa the age of seven; all other extant sources
place him among those who educate ephebes (young men of
about eighteen, one of whose main tasks was garrison duty).
In itself, this is not a conclusive reason against assigning the work to Plato, but taken together with Socrates'
description of the ephebes' training, it forms part of the
evidence for late authorship.  For example, the expression
ἐγγράφεσθαι εἰς ἐφήβους (367A), is not found among authors
of the fifth and fourth centuries, and Aristotle (*Ath. Pol.*
42) mentions only an ἐγγράφεσθαι εἰς τοὺς δήμοτας.  Moreover, when the *Axiochus'* author mentions the Council of the
Areopagus' superintendence over the young (also 367A), he
describes a situation which ceased to exist in the fourth
century.  In the *Athenian Constitution* (chap. 42) dealing
with the instruction of the ephebes, there is no mention of
the Areopagus' surveillance.  Only later, under Roman domi-
nation, does the Areopagus gain its former importance.[25]

C.  Philosophical Evidence

Further evidence against Platonic authorship and in
favor of a date after Epicurus is found in the "borrowings"
of the *Axiochus* from the works of both philosophers. First,
Feddersen followed by Chevalier noted a number of phrases
or expressions apparently taken from Plato.[26] Some are, of
course, more obviously "borrowings" than others, e.g. *Axiochus* 372A (ψυχὴ ἅπασα ἀθάνατος) is almost identical with
*Phdr*. 245C (ψυχὴ πᾶσα ἀθάνατος), whereas, e.g. *Ax*. 365B
(οὐκ ἐπιλογιῇ τὴν φύσιν...ὅτι...παρεπιδημία τίς ἐστιν ὁ
βίος) expresses, but in different language, much the same
idea as *Ap*. 40E (εἰ δ'αὖ οἷον ἀποδημῆσαί ἐστιν ὁ θάνατος
ἐνθένδε εἰς ἄλλον τόπον...). Chevalier's judgment, however,
that the author of the *Axiochus* not only imitated Plato,
but also plagiarized and plundered his work, is much too
strong, for it rests on the assumption that the *Axiochus* is,
indeed, posterior, thus perhaps begging the question of its
date and authorship.[27]

Second and perhaps more significant for dating the
*Axiochus* are the "borrowings" from Epicurus. If, for example, the *Letter to Menoeceus* (D.L. 10.139; cf. *Sent*. 2
apud D.L. 10.139) is compared with *Ax*. 365D and 369B-C, it
is hard to believe that there is only chance resemblance.
In these passages, both Epicurus and Socrates develop the
same theme; "death is nothing to us" (ὁ θάνατος οὐδὲν πρὸς
ἡμᾶς). Since death is a lapse into total insensibility, it
is foolish to fear it. Death is only painful in prospect,
not when it happens. As regards the living, death exists
not, while the dead no longer exist.

But is the borrower of these beliefs Epicurus, or the
author of the *Axiochus*? Now Sextus Empiricus (*P*. 3.229,
and *M*. 1.285) strongly implies that Epicurus first promul-
gated or demonstrated (ἀποδέδεικται) the proposition, "death
is nothing to us." Moreover, the Epicurean conception of
death as complete annihilation is not really in harmony with
Socrates' conviction that the soul is immortal. It is, as

Souilhé rightly remarked, "an awkward addition" to the pre-
vailing thought of the dialogue.[28]

In general, the *Axiochus* seems only a "mosaic of diverse and inconsistent elements,"[29] and its teachings sometimes agree neither with those of Plato nor with those of
Epicurus. Several examples can be found.[30] One is at 365E,
where Socrates refers to the human being (ἄνθρωπος) as a
union of body *and* soul (σύγκρισις) which is dissolved by
death. The soul then goes to its proper or rightful place,
but the body, being earthy and irrational, is not the human
being, for "we are soul," locked in a mortal prison. The
doctrine is, of course, not Epicurus', although Sextus Empiricus refers a similar notion to the Epicureans who say
that "we are compounded of soul and body, and death is a
dissolution of soul and body." Yet the composition is such
that "when we exist, death does not exist (for we are being
dissolved), but when death exists we do not exist. For
when the compound (σύστασις) of soul and body no longer
exists, we too cease to exist" (*P*. 3.229). But neither
does Socrates' belief expressed at 365E agree wholly with
that of Plato. For although Plato thought of the soul as a
sort of mixture (see *R*. 10.611B; *Phdr*. 246B, and *Ti*. 32C),
he never apparently considered the human person a mixture
(σύγκρισις) of body *and* soul. For him, the human person *is*
the soul (*Phd*. 66B), and death is only the separation of
two basically different things, i.e. soul and body.

There are still other passages of the *Axiochus* not in
keeping either with doctrines of Plato or of Epicurus. One
is at 370C, where the distinction is made between the *psychē*
and *pneuma*, and the latter term is used to designate something in the soul, such that it would not have been possible
for the soul (*psychē*) to undertake great endeavors, e.g. the
taming of beasts, sea faring, constructing houses, studying
the heavens, "unless a divine *pneuma* were really present in
the soul" (εἰ μή τι θεῖον ὄντως ἐνῆν πνεῦμα τῇ ψυχῇ). Such
a notion of *pneuma* seems to have been unknown to Plato, and

also certainly not part of Epicurean belief. Another non-
Platonic and non-Epicurean concept is at 371C where the
expression ἀγαθὸς δαίμων is used, implying a distinction
between good and bad *daimones*. Plato had, of course, a
daimonology, but he nowhere expressed an explicit belief in
bad *daimones*. That is first found in the teaching of his
successor Xenocrates, who postulated two species of *daimones*
corresponding to two distinct natures in us: νοῦς and ψυχή.
Εὐδαίμων is he whose *daimon* is good; κακοδαίμων is he whose
*daimon* is bad.[31] And daimonology certainly was not a part
of Epicurean doctrine.[32] To be sure, beliefs about the
gods are as valuable to the wise as false beliefs are harm-
ful to the foolish, but the gods remain passive and unin-
volved observers of the human scene.

In general, the *Axiochus* is a syncretistic work, and
doctrines inconsistent with those of Plato and of Epicurus,
not to mention with one another, are probably explained by
the author's apparent knowledge and use of the teachings of
other philosophical schools, especially those of Cynicism
and Stoicism.

*Cynic Elements.* Many scholars have noticed great
similarity between certain passages of the *Axiochus* and
several fragments of the Cynic moralists of the third century.[33] By comparison of vocabulary and themes, likely
borrowings from Crates and from Bion can be shown. First,
the passage on the miseries of life and especially those of
the young (366D,E), seems only a reworking of Teles' resumé
of Crates on human suffering.

> If it is necessary to measure the happy life
> from an excess of pleasure, no one, says Crates,
> can really be happy. Indeed, if anyone wants to
> add up all the stages in his whole life, he will
> find that troubles are far more numerous....
> If he escapes the nurse, there to grab him
> in turn are the tutor, the physical education
> teacher, the grammar teacher, the music teacher....
> Here comes the teacher of mathematics, of geome-
> try.... (By all of these he is beaten)....

> Now he is a youth: Again he fears the magis-
> trate in charge of youths, the physical education
> teacher, the teacher of weaponry, the master of
> the gymnasium.... 
> He's become a man and is in his prime: he
> serves in the army, goes on embassies for the
> state, serves as a politician....He considers the
> life he lived as a boy to be happy.... 
> He's past his prime and approaching old age:
> again he submits to being waited on like a child
> and longs for his youth.... (O'Neil's translation,
> *Teles*, V.1 ff. [49H-51H])

Second, the description of declining old age (367B) is
similar to one given by Bion of Borysthenes as reported by
Teles.

> "Just as we are ejected from our house,"
> says Bion, "when the landlord, because he has not
> received his rent, takes away the door, takes away
> the pottery, stops up the well, in the same way,"
> he says, "am I being ejected from this poor body
> when Nature, the landlady, takes away my ears, my
> hands, my feet...." (O'Neil's translation, *Teles*,
> II.149 [15H-16H])

*Stoic Elements*.  Stoic beliefs and expressions can
also be found in the *Axiochus*.  For example, the expression
εἰς τὸ χρεὼν ἰέναι (364C, 365B) seems to refer to an idea
common among the Stoics, e.g. Seneca (*Cons. Polyb*. 29),
namely, that human life is ruled by fate (εἱμαρμένη) which
is identical with nature (φύσις).  The words addressed by
Socrates to Axiochus (365A: "where are your former boasts,
and those perpetual praises of manly virtues, and that unbreakable courage...") also remind one of the dying Seneca's
farewell in Tacitus (*Ann*. 15.62).

> At the same time, now by persuasion and now by re-
> buke, he led them from tears to fortitude, asking
> them repeatedly, "where are those philosophical
> precepts, where the logic you have so long studied
> for just such an event...."

Still other passages, e.g. 366A where the soul, spread
throughout the pores of the body (ᾶτε παρεσπαρμένη τοῖς
πόροις), suffers greatly and thus longs for the heavenly

aether to which it is akin (σύμφυλον αἰθέρα), or 370B-E,
where man's possession of a divine *pneuma* and its gifts are
described, recall beliefs current among the Stoics since
Posidonius, and which were often expressed by authors of
the Roman period, e.g. Cicero, Philo of Alexandria, Seneca.

Conclusion

The previous discussion of the philosophical evidence
for the origin of the *Axiochus* has shown that its author
was familiar with Platonic, Epicurean, Cynic, and Stoic
doctrines, and incorporates them into his work.  Such a
melange seems strange at first glance.  Yet if one keeps in
mind that a similar appropriation of doctrines was typical
of the Middle Platonists who, for example, drew from the
Peripatetics and Stoics in an attempt "to express better
what Plato had really meant to say,"[34] it is not unlikely
that the author of the *Axiochus* belonged to this period or
school of philosophy.  Moreover, the Alexandrian Platonists
had abandoned the ideal of happiness as "life in accord
with nature" and turned to a more spiritual ideal of "likeness to God" (ὁμοίωσις θεῷ).  Certainly such a theme is
found in the *Axiochus* with its notion that there is a "divine spirit" in us (370) and that we are the offspring of
the gods (371D).  Our soul longs for its native heavenly
place (366), and this world in which we live is a place of
change, decay, and pain.  To be sure, these were common-
places in the ancient world, but the syncretism of the dialogue combined with its notion of "likeness to God" is con-
sistent with the Middle Platonists.  Even the Epicurean
elements in the dialogue can be understood in light of
Middle Platonism.  Since for a Platonist "it is always
open season for Epicureans,"[35] something of their position seems presented only to be ultimately rejected in the
latter part of the *Axiochus*, especially in its concluding
myth.

IV.  Literary Genre

A number of treatises in antiquity were concerned with
the same topic as the *Axiochus*, and had such titles as Περὶ
θανάτου or Περὶ πένθους, e.g. Xenocrates' Περὶ θανάτου
(D.L. 4.12) or Theophrastus' Καλλισθένης ἢ περὶ πένθους
(D.L. 5.44).[36] Most of them no longer exist, but thanks
to borrowings from them by Cicero (*Tusc.*) and Plutarch
(*Consol. ad Apoll.*), it is possible to know the usual
themes which perhaps go back to Plato's *Apology* (40C) where
Socrates claims that death is a good since it is one of two
things: (1) either it is a state of nothingness, like the
deepest sleep imaginable; or (2) it is a departure from
this life, a passage of the soul from Here to There.  These
two notions, either separately, or sometimes in unison,
seem to have been developed by authors of consolations.

The most celebrated author of consolations in antiquity
was Crantor, a member of the Academy, who lived from the end
of the fourth to the middle of the third century B.C.  He
may, in fact, have created this literary genre.  Without
doubt, his Περὶ πένθους ("On Grief") became the model for
all consolations.  Although the work no longer exists, the
use made of it by Cicero in his *Tusculanae Disputationes*
and Plutarch in his *Consolatio ad Apollonium* permits a par-
tial reconstruction.[37] It was written for Hippocles to
console him on the death of his children, and in his work
Crantor seems to have presented two opposed beliefs, namely,
the total annihilation of the soul with the loss of all
sensation, and the immortality of the soul with the joys of
a future life.  Crantor also discussed other topics, e.g.
the ills of human existence, the benefits of death which
release one from these ills, the necessity of doing away
with the passions, and submitting oneself to destiny.  It
was, according to Cicero (*Acad.* II.44,135) a "best seller."

> We have all read the Old Academician Crantor's
> *On Grief*, for it is not a large but a golden little
> volume, and one to be thoroughly studied word for
> word, as Panaetius enjoins upon Tubero. (H. Rack-
> ham, trans.)

On the whole, the content of Crantor's Περὶ πένθους seems
to have been similar to that of the *Axiochus*, and a number
of scholars have argued for Crantor's influence on the
pseudo-Plato.  For example, it is very possible that the
two stories of Agamedes and Trophonius, and the sons of the
Argive priestess (367C-D) reported also by Plutarch (*Consol.
ad Apoll.* 108E,F, 109A) and Cicero (*Tusc.* I.47,113-114)
all come from the same source, namely, Crantor's work.
Again, the notion that the insensibility brought about by
death is no different from that before birth is found in
*Axiochus* 365 (cf. 396C) which is similar to Plutarch (*Consol. ad Apoll.* 365, 109F) who maintains that as nothing was
either good or evil for us before birth, even so it will be
for us after death; or to Cicero (*Tusc.* I.37-38) with his
claim that as nothing affected us before birth, so nothing
will affect us after death.  Because of the similarity between these passages, it is likely that the common source
is Crantor.  Aside, however, from the probable influence of
Crantor on the *Axiochus*, it is clear that the dialogue is
an example of the many literary consolations composed in
antiquity.

V.  Date and Authorship of the *Axiochus*

    In view of the various evidence discussed previously,
it seems fairly certain that the *Axiochus* was written after
the rise of major philosophies of the Hellenistic period:
Epicureanism, Stoicism, and Cynicism.  Moreover, if it is
true that Crantor's famous consolation influenced the author, a date after the middle of the third century B.C.
seems quite likely.  The *Axiochus'* language, vocabulary and
syntax also points to the second-first centuries B.C., and

there seem to be no good reasons to reject the views of
Chevalier and Souilhé.  In general, the dialogue is char-
acteristic of the syncretism which preceded and continued
into the Christian era.

    The author was certainly not Plato.  But how did the
dialogue come to be attributed to him?  Immisch and Souilhé
have helped to answer this question.  With perhaps some
exaggeration, Immisch argued that the *Axiochus* was directed
against Epicureanism, and provides evidence of a polemic
between the Academy and the Garden.  And as Souilhé noticed,
the arguments that death is only the loss of all sensibility
(Epicurean), and that the soul is immortal (Platonic), do
not have the same importance or value for the dialogue's
author.[38]  The belief that death results in total unaware-
ness makes no impression on Axiochus who considers it only
the current chatter of the times, indeed, nonsense (φλυαρολογία) concocted for the young (369D).  The belief that the
soul is immortal, however, almost immediately comforts
Axiochus.  Now the soul's immortality and the prospects of
a future life are views most commonly associated with Plato,
and thus Souilhé concluded that the *Axiochus'* author was an
Academician of the first century B.C., "more rhetorician
than philosopher, as seen by his predilection for unusual,
affected words, and his concern for literary style at the
expense of a natural and genuine psychology."[39]  Moreover,
pseudo-Plato seems to have drawn much from Crantor's work,
and Crantor was one of the principal scholars of the Academy.
In view of these considerations, the *Axiochus'* assignmant
to the *corpus platonicum* is explained.

NOTES

PREFACE AND INTRODUCTION

[1] For the possible influence of de Mornay on Spenser, and English interest in the former's *Discours de la vie et de la mort*, including the *Axiochus*, see F. M. Padelford's introduction to the facsimile edition of Spenser's translation of the *Axiochus*: *The Axiochus of Plato Translated by Edmund Spenser* (Baltimore: Johns Hopkins, 1934). Spenser's lost work was discovered in 1931 at a sale by W. Heffer and Sons. Despite his knowledge of Spenser's work, Blakeney remarks "the present edition of the *Axiochus* is (I believe) the first to be published in this country."

[2] For an annotated bibliography of editions and translations of the *Axiochus*, see Chevalier (*Etude critique du dialogue pseudo-platonicien l'Axiochos* [Paris: F. Alcan, 1915] 2-8).

[3] Ficino's Latin translation of the *Axiochus*, following his treatise, *De religione christiana et fidei pietate*, was entitled *Xenocrates, de morte contemnenda*.

[4] See Blakeney's preface to his translation of the *Axiochus*: *The Axiochus: On Death and Immortality* (London: F. Muller, 1937).

[5] See, for example, Chevalier (*Etude critique*, 131) who paradoxically maintains that the principal interest of the *Axiochus* resides in its absence of originality, both in form and content. See also the disparaging remarks of Taylor (*Plato: The Man and his Work* [New York: Meridian, 1956] 550-52) or of Heidel (*Pseudo-Platonica* [Baltimore, 1896; reprint, New York: Arno, 1976] 18) who finds the dialogue "uncritically eclectic." The very recent opinion of W. K. C. Guthrie is not much different. He remarks that Socrates offers Axiochus a consolation which is a "scarcely reconciliable mixture of Platonic with what sounds like Epicurean teaching." Nonetheless he believes that if the work "does not much concern the student of Plato as such, it it has some interest for the historian of religion." What this may be, he does not state (see Guthrie, *A History of Greek Philosophy* [5 vols.; Cambridge: Cambridge University, 1962-1978] 5.395).

[6] On *sōma-sēma*, see Guthrie (*The Greeks and their Gods* [Boston: Beacon, 1954] 311 n. 3). For somewhat extensive discussion on the relationship of the Orphics to the Pythagoreans, see Burkert, *Lore and Science in Ancient Pythagoreanism* ([trans. E. L. Minar, Jr.; Cambridge, MA: Harvard, 1972] 125ff.) and especially his *Griechische Religion der archaischen und klassischen Epoche* (= *Die Religionen der Menschheit* XV [Stuttgart: W. Kohlhammer, 1977] 440-47) on

23

Orpheus and Pythagoras and the difficulties of distinguish-
ing doctrines of their followers. See also Guthrie, *History*, 1.150 and 198f.

[7]On Plato's relationship to Orphism, see Guthrie,
*Orpheus and Greek Religion* ([2nd ed.; London: Methuen,
1952] 238-44) and Burkert, *Griechische Religion* (444).

[8]Immisch, *Philologische Studien zu Plato*, Vol. 1:
*Axiochus* (Leipzig: B. G. Teubner, 1896) 31ff. His view is
shared by Taylor among others.

[9]E. Schweizer (*TDNT*, s.v. πνεῦμα) has an excellent
survey of the various meanings and uses of the term in
natural science and philosophy (352-57). The concept was
especially important in Stoic thought (cf. Seneca, *Ep.*
66.12) where the divine spirit has its seat in human reason:
"reason (*ratio*) is nothing other than a part of the divine
spirit (*divini spiritus*) thrust in the human body."
Schweizer refers to the concept of the *divine pneuma* in the
*Axiochus* on page 338 citing καθαρὸν δίκαιον...πνεῦμα θεοῦ
σωτῆρος (*Collection of Ancient Greek Inscriptions in the
British Museum* IV.2 [1916] 1062) or the πνεῦμα θεοῦ which
may even conceive in a human woman (Plutarch, *Num.* 4.6).
The Stoic parallels seem much closer; on the *pneuma* in the
human soul, see also Plutarch (*De def. or.* 432D) and note
57 to my translation.

[10]Shorey's translation, *Loeb Classical Library*; cf.
Kern, *Orphicorum Fragmenta* ([Berlin: Weidmann, 1922; re-
print, 1963] iv, 83). Shorey suggests the son is "possibly
Eumolpus."

[11]See Mylonas, *Eleusis and the Eleusinian Mysteries*
(Princeton: Princeton University, 1961) pages 213 and 316
for the initiation of Dionysus, and 205-208 and passim for
the initiation of Heracles.

[12]For discussion of the vase-paintings, see ibid.,
211-13.

[13]Nilsson, *Geschichte der griechischen Religion*, Vol.
2: *Die hellenistische und römische Zeit* (= *Handbuch der
Altertumswissenschaft* V.2.2) (2nd ed.; Munich: Beck, 1961)
2.242. Nilsson makes this remark in connection with the
"wissenschaftliche Deutung" of the underworld, primarily
the reference to the spherical universe at *Ax.* 371A.

[14]Chevalier, *Etude critique*, 111-13.

[15]Chevalier, assuming the dialogue antedates the first
century A.D., explained the similarities as the result of
the interaction between Hellenism and Judaism near the end
of the Alexandrian period (ibid., 114).

[16]Ibid., 117ff.  Chevalier also provides useful bibliographical references in his notes.

[17]The passages from Montaigne, Fabricius, and Meiners are quoted by Chevalier (ibid., 129-30).

[18]Ibid., 11-13, and Souilhé, *Axiochus*, 118-19.

[19]Souilhé, *Axiochus*, 125.

[20]Shorey, *What Plato Said* (Chicago: University of Chicago, 1968) 437.

[21]For criticisms and summaries of Buresch's views, see Chevalier (*Etude critique*, 25-29) and Souilhé (*Axiochus*, 124-25).

[22]The views of these scholars are found in their works listed in the bibliography.

[23]See Chevalier's study of the vocabulary (*Etude critique*, 43-66); see also Souilhé's observations on style (*Axiochus*, 125-26).

[24]Chevalier, *Etude critique*, 63.

[25]For this discussion of the historical evidence of the ephebes and Areopagus, I am indebted to Chevalier (*Etude critique*, 31-35) and to Souilhé (*Axiochus*, 126-27).

[26]H. Feddersen, *Über den pseudoplatonischen Dialog Axiochus* (Programm Cuxhaven: G. Rauschenplat, 1895) 22-29, and Chevalier, *Etude critique*, 67-70.

[27]Chevalier, *Etude critique*, 70.

[28]Souilhé, *Axiochus*, 129.

[29]Chevalier, *Etude critique*, 21.

[30]Examples are given by Chevalier (ibid., 17-20) and Souilhé (*Axiochus*, 129-30).

[31]See Chevalier (*Etude critique*, 19-20) and the recent treatment of Xenocrates in J. Dillon, *The Middle Platonists* ([London: G. Duckworth, 1977] 22-39, esp. 30-32).

[32]If one has false beliefs about the gods, evils can arise from them, since they could not occur if mortals did not know that the gods existed.  On Epicurus' religious beliefs, see A. J. Festugière, *Epicurus and his Gods* (Cambridge, MA: Harvard, 1956) and J. M. Rist, *Epicurus: An Introduction* ([Cambridge: Cambridge University, 1972] 140-63).

[33]For example, Feddersen, *Über den pseudoplatonischen Dialog Axiochus*, 13-15; Chevalier, *Etude critique*, 82-83; Souilhé, 132.

[34]The remark is by J. Dillon (*The Middle Platonists*, xiv) to whose work I am indebted for the concluding observations. On the importance of "likeness to God," see 44 and 192.

[35]Ibid., 242.

[36]The major study on consolations in antiquity is that of C. Buresch. For a brief summary of the literary genre, see J. Hani, *Plutarque. Consolation à Apollonios* (= *Etudes et Commentaires* 78) ([Paris: Klincksieck, 1972] 11).

[37]See, for example, Souilhé, *Axiochus*, 122-23, 130-31.

[38]Souilhé, *Axiochus*, 135.

[39]Ibid., 135-36. Souilhé's judgment is not novel. It goes back to Susemihl and others; see Chevalier, *Etude critique*, 106 n. 1.

TEXT AND TRANSLATION

ΑΞΙΟΧΟΣ

[ἢ περὶ θανάτου.]

ΣΩΚΡΑΤΗΣ ΚΛΕΙΝΙΑΣ ΑΞΙΟΧΟΣ

ΣΩ. Ἐξιόντι μοι ἐς Κυνόσαργες καὶ γενομένῳ     364a
μοι κατὰ τὸν Ἰλισὸν διῆξε φωνή βοῶντός του,
"Σώκρατες, Σώκρατες". Ὡς δὲ ἐπιστραφεὶς περιεσκό-
πουν ὁπόθεν εἴη, Κλεινίαν ὁρῶ τὸν Ἀξιόχου θέοντα ἐπὶ
Καλλιρρόην μετὰ Δάμωνος τοῦ μουσικοῦ καὶ Χαρμίδου τοῦ
Γλαύκωνος· ἤστην δὲ αὐτῷ ὁ μὲν διδάσκαλος τῶν κατὰ
μουσικήν, ὁ δ' ἐξ ἑταιρείας ἐραστὴς ἅμα καὶ ἐρώμενος.
Ἐδόκει οὖν μοι ἀφεμένῳ τῆς εὐθὺ ὁδοῦ ἀπαντᾶν αὐτοῖς,     b
ὅπως ῥᾷστα ὁμοῦ γενοίμεθα. Δεδακρυμένος δὲ ὁ Κλεινίας,
"Σώκρατες," ἔφη, "νῦν ὁ καιρὸς ἐνδείξασθαι τὴν ἀεὶ
θρυλουμένην πρὸς σοῦ σοφίαν· ὁ γὰρ πατὴρ ἔκ τινος ὥρας
αἰφνιδίου ἀδυνάτως ἔχει καὶ πρὸς τῷ τέλει τοῦ βίου
ἐστίν, ἀνιαρῶς τε φέρει τὴν τελευτήν, καίτοι γε τὸν
πρόσθεν χρόνον διαχλευάζων τοὺς μορμολυττομένους τὸν
θάνατον καὶ πρᾴως ἐπιτωθάζων. Ἀφικόμενος οὖν     c
παρηγόρησον αὐτὸν ὡς εἴωθας, ὅπως ἀστενακτὶ ἐς τὸ
χρεὼν ἴῃ, καί μοι σὺν τοῖς λοιποῖς ἵνα καὶ τοῦτο
εὐσεβηθῇ". "Ἀλλ' οὐκ ἀτυχήσεις μου, ὦ Κλεινία,
οὐδενὸς τῶν μετρίων, καὶ ταῦτα ἐφ' ὅσια παρακαλῶν.
Ἐπειγώμεθα δ' οὖν· εἰ γὰρ οὕτως ἔχει, ὠκύτητος δεῖ".

ΚΛ. Ὀφθέντος σου μόνον, ὦ Σώκρατες, ῥαΐσει·
καὶ γὰρ ἤδη πολλάκις αὐτῷ γέγονε συμπτώματος ἀνασφῆλαι.

# AXIOCHUS

## (or concerning death)

### SOCRATES   CLEINIAS   AXIOCHUS

SOCRATES:  While I was going to the Cynosarges       364A
and nearing the Ilisus, the voice of someone shouting
"Socrates, Socrates" reached me.[1]  And when I turned
around and tried to find its source, I saw Cleinias,
Axiochus' son, running toward the Callirrhoe together
with Damon, the musician, and Charmides, the son of
Glaucon:[2] of these, Damon was Cleinias' music teacher,
and the other on terms of intimate friendship, at
once lover and beloved.  I then decided to turn from       B
the road right away to meet them so that we might get
together as quickly as possible.  And Cleinias with
tears in his eyes said, "Socrates, now is the chance
to show your much talked about wisdom;[3] for my father
is incapacitated by a sudden illness,[4] and is at the
end of his life.  And wretchedly he endures his end,
even though in times past he simply scoffed at those
who were scared of death, and gently poked fun at
them.[5]  So come and console him in your usual way,       C
that he may meet his fate without complaint,[6] and so
that this can be dealt with in a reverent way by me
and the others as well."[7]  "Well, you will not find
me, Cleinias, refusing so reasonable a request,
especially as these matters to which you summon me
pertain to religion.  Let us go then; for if the
situation is like this, speed is essential."

CLEINIAS:  The very sight of you, Socrates, will
strengthen him.  For often before he has managed to
recover from such an attack.

ΣΩ. 'Ως δὲ θᾶττον τὴν παρὰ τὸ τεῖχος ᾔειμεν          364d
ταῖς 'Ιτωνίαις--πλησίον γὰρ ᾤκει τῶν πυλῶν πρὸς τῇ       365a
'Αμαζονίδι στήλῃ--καταλαμβάνομεν αὐτὸν ἤδη μὲν συνει-
λεγμένον τὰς ἀφὰς καὶ τῷ σώματι ῥωμαλέον, ἀσθενῆ δὲ
τὴν ψυχήν, πάνυ ἐνδεᾶ παραμυθίας, πολλάκις δὲ ἀνα-
φερόμενον καὶ στεναγμοὺς ἱέντα σὺν δακρύοις καὶ
κροτήσεσι χειρῶν. Κατιδὼν δὲ αὐτόν, "'Αξίοχε, τί
ταῦτα"; ἔφην· "ποῦ τὰ πρόσθεν αὐχήματα καὶ αἱ συνεχεῖς
εὐλογίαι τῶν ἀρετῶν καὶ τὸ ἄρρατον ἐν σοὶ θάρσος; ὡς
γὰρ ἀγωνιστὴς δειλός, ἐν τοῖς γυμνασίοις γενναῖος
φαινόμενος, ὑπολέλοιπας ἐν τοῖς ἄθλοις. Οὐκ ἐπιλογιῇ      b
τὴν φύσιν περιεσκεμμένως, ἀνὴρ τοσόσδε τῷ χρόνῳ καὶ
κατήκοος λόγων, καὶ εἰ μηδὲν ἕτερον, 'Αθηναῖος, ὅτι,
τὸ κοινὸν δὴ τοῦτο καὶ πρὸς ἀπάντων θρυλούμενον, παρεπιδημία τίς ἐστιν ὁ βίος, καὶ ὅτι δεῖ ἐπιεικῶς διαγα-
γόντας εὐθύμως μόνον οὐχὶ παιανίζοντας εἰς τὸ χρεὼν
ἀπιέναι; τὸ δὲ οὕτως μαλακῶς καὶ δυσαποσπάστως ἔχειν
νηπίου δίκην οὐ περὶ φρονοῦσαν ἡλικίαν ἔχειν;"

ΑΞ. 'Αληθῆ ταῦτα, ὦ Σώκρατες, καὶ ὀρθῶς μοι         c
φαίνῃ λέγων· ἀλλ' οὐκ οἶδα ὅπως παρ' αὐτό μοι τὸ
δεινὸν γενομένῳ οἱ μὲν καρτεροὶ καὶ περιττοὶ λόγοι
ὑπεκπνέουσι λεληθότως καὶ ἀτιμάζονται, ἀντίσχει δὲ
δέος τι, ποικίλως περιαμύττον τὸν νοῦν, εἰ στερήσομαι
τοῦδε τοῦ φωτὸς καὶ τῶν ἀγαθῶν, ἀιδὴς δὲ καὶ ἄπυστος
ὁποίποτε κείσομαι σηπόμενος, εἰς εὐλὰς καὶ κνώδαλα
μεταβάλλων.

ΣΩ. Συνάπτεις γάρ, ὦ 'Αξίοχε, παρὰ τὴν ἀνεπιστα-
σίαν ἀνεπιλογίστως τῇ ἀναισθησίᾳ αἴσθησιν, καὶ σεαυτῷ       d
ὑπεναντία καὶ ποιεῖς καὶ λέγεις, οὐκ ἐπιλογιζόμενος

SOCRATES:  After hurrying along the wall to the   364D
Itonian gates--for he lived near the gates by the   365A
Amazon column--we found that Axiochus had already
recovered from his ailments, and was strong in body,
though weak in spirit.[8]  He was really in need of
consolation, often sighing deeply and emitting loud
groans together with tears and beating of hands.[9]
Looking down at him, I said, "Axiochus, what is all
this?  Where are your former boasts, and those perpetual praises of manly virtues, and that unbreakable
courage of yours?  For like a timid athlete, though
seeming brave in school exercises, you have failed in
the actual contests.  Won't you take nature into
serious consideration, you a man so advanced in age,          B
one who listens to rational arguments,[10] and if nothing else, an Athenian?  Indeed it's a commonplace,
everybody's talk, that life is a brief stay in a
foreign land,[11] and that it's necessary for those
who spent it reasonably well to meet their destiny
cheerfully, all but singing a paean of praise?  A
behavior, however, that is so faint-hearted and so
unwilling to be torn from life,[12] is proper for a
child, but not for one of mature age."

AXIOCHUS:  True enough, Socrates, I think you          C
are right.  Still I don't know why it happens that
as I get close to the grim reality, all the forceful
and extravagant arguments just blow away and become
worthless.  But a kind of fear persists.  It stings
my mind in various ways that I am to lose this light
of day and these goods,[13] that unseen and forgotten
I will lie somewhere rotting, becoming food for
worms and beasts.

SOCRATES:  But, Axiochus, because of your
thoughtlessness, you uncritically connect sensation          D
with absence of sensation; and you are doing and

ὅτι ἅμα μὲν ὀδύρῃ τὴν ἀναισθησίαν, ἅμα δὲ ἀλγεῖς ἐπὶ
σήψεσι καὶ στερήσει τῶν ἡδέων, ὥσπερ εἰς ἕτερον ζῆν
ἀποθανούμενος, ἀλλ᾽ οὐκ εἰς παντελῆ μεταβαλὼν ἀναισθησίαν καὶ τὴν αὐτὴν τῇ πρὸ τῆς γενέσεως. Ὡς οὖν ἐπὶ
τῆς Δράκοντος ἢ Κλεισθένους πολιτείας οὐδὲν περὶ σὲ
κακὸν ἦν--ἀρχὴν γὰρ οὐκ ἦς, περὶ ὃν ἂν ἦν--οὕτως οὐδὲ
μετὰ τὴν τελευτὴν γενήσεται· σὺ γὰρ οὐκ ἔσῃ περὶ ὃν     365e
ἔσται. Πάντα τοιγαροῦν τὸν τοιόνδε φλύαρον ἀποσκέδα-
σαι, τοῦτο ἐννοήσας, ὅτι τῆς συγκρίσεως ἅπαξ διαλυ-
θείσης καὶ τῆς ψυχῆς εἰς τὸν οἰκεῖον ἱδρυθείσης τόπον,
τὸ ὑπολειφθὲν σῶμα, γεῶδες ὂν καὶ ἄλογον, οὐκ ἔστιν ὁ
ἄνθρωπος. Ἡμεῖς μὲν γάρ ἐσμεν ψυχή, ζῷον ἀθάνατον
ἐν θνητῷ καθειργμένον φρουρίῳ· τὸ δὲ σκῆνος τουτὶ     366a
πρὸς κακοῦ περιήρμοσεν ἡ φύσις, ᾧ τὰ μὲν ἥδοντα
ἀμυχιαῖα καὶ πτηνὰ καὶ εἰς πλείους ὀδύνας ἀνακεκρα-
μένα, τὰ δὲ ἀλγεινὰ ἀκραιφνῆ καὶ πολυχρόνια καὶ τῶν
ἡδόντων ἄμοιρα· νόσους δὲ καὶ φλεγμονὰς τῶν αἰσθητηρίων,
ἔτι δὲ τὰς ἐντὸς κακότητας, οἷς ἀναγκαστῶς, ἅτε παρεσπαρμένη τοῖς πόροις, ἡ ψυχὴ συναλγοῦσα τὸν οὐράνιον
ποθεῖ καὶ σύμφυλον αἰθέρα, καὶ διψᾷ, τῆς ἐκεῖσε διαίτης
καὶ χορείας ὀριγνωμένη. Ὥστε ἡ τοῦ ζῆν ἀπαλλαγὴ     b
κακοῦ τινός ἐστιν εἰς ἀγαθὸν μεταβολή.

ΑΞ. Κακὸν οὖν, ὦ Σώκρατες, ἡγούμενος τὸ ζῆν πῶς
ἐν αὐτῷ μένεις; καὶ ταῦτα φροντιστὴς ὢν καὶ ὑπὲρ ἡμᾶς
τοὺς πολλοὺς τῷ νῷ διαφέρων;

saying things contrary to yourself, not realizing
that at one and the same time you lament the absence
of sensation and are pained at decay and loss of
pleasures, just as if by dying you entered into
another life instead of having lapsed into complete
insensibility such as you had before birth.[14]  So,
for example, just as in the administration of Draco
and Cleisthenes[15] there was nothing evil that concerned you--for it is elementary that you, whom the
evil could have concerned, did not exist--so not even
after death will there be any evil.  For you, whom          365E
it would concern, will not exist.  Away, then, with
all this nonsense, and realize this: that once the
union of body and soul is dissolved and the soul
has been established in its proper place, the corpse
which remains, being earthly and irrational, is not
the human person.  For we are soul,[16] an immortal
living being, locked up in a mortal prison.[17]  But        366A
Nature has fashioned this tent[18] for suffering of
evil; its pleasures are superficial and fleeting,
mixed with many pains, but its sufferings are undiluted, long lasting, without a share of pleasure.
Moreover, since the soul is spread throughout the
pores of the body,[19] it necessarily suffers, along
with the organs of sense, diseases, inflammations,
and still other internal ills.  Yet all the while
the souls yearns after and is athirst for its native
heavenly aither,[20] always striving for the life there
and the divine choral dance.  Thus the release from
this life is a change from a kind of evil to a good.[21]    B

    AXIOCHUS:  Well then, Socrates, since you
consider this life an evil, how can you remain in it?
Especially as you are a thinker about these issues,[22]
and surpass many of us in intelligence.

ΣΩ.  'Αξίοχε, σὺ δὲ οὐκ ἔτυμά μοι μαρτυρεῖς,
οἴει δὲ καθάπερ 'Αθηναίων ἡ πληθύς, ἐπειδὴ ζητητικός
εἰμι τῶν πραγμάτων, ἐπιστήμονά του εἶναί με.  'Εγὼ
δὲ εὐξαίμην ἂν τὰ κοινὰ ταῦτα εἰδέναι· τοσοῦτον
ἀποδέω τῶν περιττῶν.  Καὶ ταῦτα δὲ ἃ λέγω, Προδίκου      366c
ἐστὶ τοῦ σοφοῦ ἀπηχήματα, τὰ μὲν διμοίρου ἐωνημένα,
τὰ δὲ δυοῖν δραχμαῖν, τὰ δὲ τετραδράχμου.  Προῖκα
γὰρ ἀνὴρ οὗτος οὐδένα διδάσκει, διὰ παντὸς δὲ ἔθος
ἐστὶν αὐτῷ φωνεῖν τὸ 'Επιχάρμειον, "ἃ δὲ χεὶρ τὰν
χεῖρα νίζει"· δός τι, καὶ λάβε τι.  Καὶ πρῴην γοῦν
παρὰ Καλλίᾳ τῷ 'Ιππονίκου ποιούμενος ἐπίδειξιν τοσάδε
τοῦ ζῆν κατεῖπεν, ὥστε ἔγωγε μὲν παρὰ ἀκαρῆ διέγραψα
τὸν βίον, καὶ ἐξ ἐκείνου θανατᾷ μου ἡ ψυχή, 'Αξίοχε.

ΑΞ.  Τίνα δὲ ἦν τὰ λεχθέντα;

ΣΩ.  Φράσαιμι ἄν σοι ταῦτα ἃ μνημονεύσω.  "Εφη        d
γάρ, Τί μέρος τῆς ἡλικίας ἄμοιρον τῶν ἀνιαρῶν; οὐ
κατὰ μὲν τὴν πρώτην γένεσιν τὸ νήπιον κλάει, τοῦ ζῆν
ἀπὸ λύπης ἀρχόμενον; οὐ λείπεται γοῦν οὐδεμιᾶς
ἀλγηδόνος, ἀλλ' ἢ δι' ἔνδειαν ἢ περιψυγμὸν ἢ θάλπος
ἢ πληγὴν ὀδυνᾶται, λαλῆσαι μὲν οὔπω δυνάμενον ἃ πάσχει,
κλαυθμυριζόμενον δὲ καὶ ταύτην τῆς δυσαρεστήσεως μίαν
ἔχον φωνήν.  'Οπόταν δὲ εἰς τὴν ἑπταετίαν ἀφίκηται
πολλοὺς πόνους διαντλῆσαν, ἐπέστησαν παιδαγωγοὶ καὶ        e
γραμματισταὶ καὶ παιδοτρίβαι τυραννοῦντες· αὐξανομένου
δὲ κριτικοί, γεωμέτραι, τακτικοί, πολὺ πλῆθος δεσπο-
τῶν.  'Επειδὰν δὲ εἰς τοὺς ἐφήβους ἐγγραφῇ, κοσμητὴς
καὶ φόβος χειρῶν, ἔπειτα Λύκειον καὶ 'Ακαδήμεια καὶ        367a
γυμνασίαρχοι καὶ ῥάβδοι καὶ κακῶν ἀμετρίαι·

   SOCRATES: Axiochus, in my opinion you are not a reliable witness, but like the Athenian people, you think that because I'm devoted to looking into human affairs, I have some expertise. But I often wish that I knew these ordinary matters, so far am I from the extraordinary.[23] My remarks are but echoes of     366C the wise Prodicus, "some purchased for a half drachma, others for two, and still others for four."[24] For this man instructs no one free of charge, and it is his habit to repeat constantly the saying of Epicharmus, "one hand washes the other: give something and take something."[25] In any case, he recently gave a grand speech at the house of Callias, son of Hipponicus,[26] and said so much against "living," that I came within a hair's breadth of writing off life altogether. And ever since, Axiochus, my soul has longed for death.[27]

   AXIOCHUS: What did he say?

   SOCRATES: I can tell you what I remember. For     D he said, What part of a lifetime is without its portion of griefs?[28] Doesn't the infant cry out at the first moment of birth, beginning his life with distress? Certainly he lacks no suffering, but because of need, cold or heat, or a beating, he is distressed: he cannot yet tell what he is suffering, but only by the sound of his crying can he express his displeasure. When he reaches the age of seven, having endured many troubles, tyrannizing tutors, elementary school teachers, and physical trainers set upon him;[29] and as he grows, there are language teachers, geometry teachers, military instructors,[30] all a great crowd of despots. When he is enrolled among the Ephebes, there comes the director, and fear of beatings;[31] then the Lyceum and the Academy,[32] superintendants of the Gymnasium with their sticks     367A and miseries without measure.

καὶ πᾶς ὁ τοῦ μειρακίσκου χρόνος ἐστὶν ὑπὸ σωφρονισ-
τὰς καὶ τὴν ἐπὶ τοὺς νέους αἵρεσιν τῆς ἐξ Ἀρείου
πάγου βουλῆς. Ἐπειδὰν δὲ ἀπολυθῇ τούτων, φροντίδες
ἄντικρυς ὑπέδυσαν καὶ διαλογισμοὶ τίνα τις τοῦ βίου
ὁδὸν ἐνστήσεται, καὶ τοῖς ὕστερον χαλεποῖς ἐφάνη τὰ
πρῶτα παιδιὰ καὶ νηπίων ὡς ἀληθῶς φόβητρα· στρατεῖαί
τε γὰρ καὶ τραύματα καὶ συνεχεῖς ἀγῶνες. Εἶτα λαθὸν      367b
ὑπῆλθε τὸ γῆρας, εἰς ὃ πᾶν συρρεῖ τὸ τῆς φύσεως
ἐπίκηρον καὶ δυσαλθές. Κἂν μή τις θᾶττον ὡς χρέος
ἀποδιδῷ τὸ ζῆν, ὡς ὀβολοστάτις ἡ φύσις ἐπιστᾶσα
ἐνεχυράζει τοῦ μὲν ὄψιν, τοῦ δὲ ἀκοήν, πολλάκις δὲ
ἄμφω. Κἂν ἐπιμείνῃ τις, παρέλυσεν, ἐλωβήσατο,
παρήρθρωσεν. Ἄλλοι πολυγήρως ἀκμάζουσι, καὶ τῷ νῷ
δὶς παῖδες οἱ γέροντες γίγνονται. Διὰ τοῦτο καὶ οἱ
θεοὶ τῶν ἀνθρωπείων ἐπιστήμονες, οὓς ἂν περὶ πλείστου      c
ποιῶνται, θᾶττον ἀπαλλάττουσι τοῦ ζῆν. Ἀγαμήδης
γοῦν καὶ Τροφώνιος οἱ δειμάμενοι τὸ Πυθοῖ τοῦ θεοῦ
τέμενος, εὐξάμενοι τὸ κράτιστον αὐτοῖς γενέσθαι,
κοιμηθέντες οὐκέτ' ἀνέστησαν· οἵ τε τῆς Ἀργείας
[Ἥρας] ἱερείας υἱεῖς, ὁμοίως εὐξαμένης αὐτοῖς τῆς
μητρὸς γενέσθαι τι τῆς εὐσεβείας παρὰ τῆς Ἥρας γέρας,
ἐπειδὴ τοῦ ζεύγους ὑστερήσαντος ὑποδύντες αὐτοὶ
διήνεγκαν αὐτὴν εἰς τὸν νεών, μετὰ τὴν εὐχὴν νυκτὶ
μετήλλαξαν. Μακρὸν ἂν εἴη διεξιέναι τὰ τῶν ποιητῶν,      d
οἳ στόμασι θειοτέροις τὰ περὶ τὸν βίον θεσπιῳδοῦσιν,
ὡς κατοδύρονται τὸ ζῆν· ἑνὸς δὲ μόνου μνησθήσομαι
τοῦ ἀξιολογωτάτου, λέγοντος--

So his entire youth is spent under superintendents
and the committee chosen by the council of the Areopagus to deal with the young.[33]  When freed from these
matters, worries immediately creep upon him and delib-
erations about the career one is to pursue.  But compared with the later troubles, those of earlier years
appeared trivial--only the nightmares of children--
I mean, for example, military campaigns, wounds, and
continual contests.

Then old age creeps upon him unawares, into          367B
which flows all in nature that is mortal and perishable.[34]  And unless one quickly pays back living,
like a debt, nature stands by like a money lender,[35]
taking security, sight from one, from another hearing,
and often both.  And if someone resists, nature
paralyzes, mutilates, or dislocates limbs.  Others
remain physically vigorous in old age, but in mind
those old people undergo a second childhood.[36]  That
is why the gods, who understand human affairs, quickly
release from life those whom they consider of great-         C
est worth.[37]  For example, Agamedes and Trophonius,
who built the sacred precinct of the god at Pytho,[38]
after praying that the best might happen to them,
fell asleep and never awakened again.  There are also
the sons of the Argive priestess whose mother prayed
for them in the same way that they might receive from
Hera some reward for their filial piety,[39] for when
the team of mules was late, the sons yoked themselves
to the cart and took her to the temple.  And that
night after their mother's prayer they passed away.
It would take too long to go through the works of          D
poets who, with voices of higher divinity, chant in
prophetic tones the affairs of life, while deploring
living itself.  I shall quote only one of them, the
most worthy who said:

ὣς γὰρ ἐπεκλώσαντο θεοὶ δειλοῖσι βροτοῖσιν,
ζώειν ἀχνυμένοις,

καὶ--

οὐ μὲν γάρ τί ποτ᾽ ἐστὶν οἰζυρώτερον ἀνδρὸς
πάντων ὅσσα τε γαῖαν ἐπιπνείει τε καὶ ἕρπει.          367e

τὸν δ᾽ Ἀμφιάραον τί φησι; --                            368a

τὸν πέρι κῆρι φίλει Ζεύς τ᾽ αἰγίοχος καὶ Ἀπόλλων
παντοίῃ φιλότητι· οὐδ᾽ ἵκετο γήραος οὐδόν.

ὁ δὲ κελεύων--

τὸν φύντα θρηνεῖν εἰς ὅσ᾽ ἔρχεται κακά,

τί σοι φαίνεται; ἀλλὰ παύομαι, μή ποτε παρὰ τὴν ὑπό-
σχεσιν μηκύνω καὶ ἐτέρων μιμνησκόμενος. Ποίαν δέ τις
ἐλόμενος ἐπιτήδευσιν ἢ τέχνην οὐ μέμφεται καὶ τοῖς
παροῦσι χαλεπαίνει; τὰς χειρωνακτικὰς ἐπέλθωμεν καὶ          b
βαναύσους, πονουμένων ἐκ νυκτὸς εἰς νύκτα, καὶ μόλις
ποριζομένων τἀπιτήδεια, κατοδυρομένων τε αὐτῶν καὶ
πᾶσαν ἀγρυπνίαν ἀναπιμπλάντων ὀλοφυρμοῦ καὶ δακρύων;
ἀλλὰ τὸν πλωτικὸν καταλεξώμεθα, περαιούμενον διὰ
τοσῶνδε κινδύνων καὶ μήτε, ὡς ἀπεφήνατο Βίας, ἐν τοῖς
τεθνηκόσιν ὄντα μήτε ἐν τοῖς βιοῦσιν; ὁ γὰρ ἐπίγειος
ἄνθρωπος ὡς ἀμφίβιος αὐτὸν εἰς τὸ πέλαγος ἔρριψεν,
ἐπὶ τῇ τύχῃ γενόμενος πᾶς. Ἀλλ᾽ ἡ γεωργία γλυκύ;          c
δῆλον· ἀλλ᾽ οὐχ ὅλον, ὥς φασιν, ἕλκος, ἀεὶ λύπης
πρόφασιν εὑρισκόμενον; κλᾶον νυνὶ μὲν αὐχμόν, νυνὶ
δὲ ἐπομβρίας, νυνὶ δὲ ἐπίκαυσιν, νυνὶ δὲ ἐρυσίβην,
νυνὶ δὲ θάλπος ἄκαιρον ἢ κρύος; ἀλλ᾽ ἡ πολυτίμητος
πολιτεία--πολλὰ γὰρ ὑπερβαίνω--

Such is the way the gods spun life for unfortunate
     mortals,
that we live in unhappiness,[40]

and--

Since among all creatures, that breathe on earth
     and crawl on it
there is not anywhere a thing more dismal than          367E
     man is.

And what does he say of Amphiaraus?[41]                         368A

Whom Zeus of the aegis loved in his heart,
     as did Apollo,
with every favor, but he never came to the
     doorsill of old age.

And he who bids us--

Weep for the newly born; he meets so many ills--[42]

what do you think of him?

But I stop now so that I do not break my promise
and lengthen the list by remembering other examples.
But what pursuit or skill has anyone chosen and not
found fault with and distress at its conditions?  Are          B
we to approach the skills of handicraftsmen and arti-
sans laboring from dawn to dusk scarcely able to provide their needs, deploring themselves and filling
all their waking hours with lamentations and fears?[43]
Well, are we to consider the merchant who sails
through so many perils and is, as Bias has shown,[44]
neither among the dead nor among the living?  For
terrestial man throws himself onto the sea as if he          C
were amphibious, and is entirely at the mercy of
chance.  Well, is farming a pleasant occupation?
Obviously![45]  Yet isn't it just one complete
blister, as they say, which always finds an excuse
for pain?  For now the farmer weeps at drought, now
at too much rain, now at blight, now at excessive heat
or frost.  Well, how about highly-prized politics--
for I skip over many things--through how many fearful

διὰ πόσων ἐλαύνεται δεινῶν, τὴν μὲν χαρὰν ἔχουσα
φλεγμονῆς δίκην παλλομένην καὶ σφυγματώδη, τὴν δὲ
ἀπότευξιν ἀλγεινὴν καὶ θανάτων μυρίων χείρω; τίς                 368d
γὰρ ἂν εὐδαιμονήσειε πρὸς ὄχλον ζῶν, εἰ ποππυσθείη
καὶ κροτηθείη δήμου παίγνιον ἐκβαλλόμενον, συριττό-
μενον, ζημιούμενον, θνῆσκον, ἐλεούμενον; ἐπεί τοί γε,
'Αξίοχε πολιτικέ, ποῦ τέθνηκε Μιλτιάδης; ποῦ δὲ
Θεμιστοκλῆς; ποῦ δ' 'Εφιάλτης; ποῦ δὲ πρῴην οἱ δέκα
στρατηγοί, ὅτ' ἐγὼ μὲν οὐκ ἐπηρόμην τὴν γνώμην;
--οὐ γὰρ ἐφαίνετό μοι σεμνὸν μαινομένῳ δήμῳ συνεξάρ-
χειν· οἱ δὲ περὶ Θηραμένην καὶ Καλλίξενον τῇ
ὑστεραίᾳ προέδρους ἐγκαθέτους ὑφέντες κατεχειρο-
τόνησαν τῶν ἀνδρῶν ἄκριτον θάνατον. Καίτοι γε σὺ            369a
μόνος αὐτοῖς ἤμυνες καὶ Εὐρυπτόλεμος, τρισμυρίων
ἐκκλησιαζόντων.

AΞ.  "Εστι ταῦτα, ὦ Σώκρατες· καὶ ἔγωγε ἐξ
ἐκείνου ἅλις ἔσχον τοῦ βήματος καὶ χαλεπώτερον οὐδὲν
ἐφάνη μοι πολιτείας. Δῆλον δὲ τοῖς ἐν τῷ ἔργῳ γενο-
μένοις. Σὺ μὲν γὰρ οὕτω λαλεῖς ὡς ἐξ ἀπόπτου θεώ-
μενος, ἡμεῖς δ' ἴσμεν ἀκριβέστερον οἱ διὰ πείρας
ἰόντες. Δῆμος γάρ, ὦ φίλε Σώκρατες, ἀχάριστον,
ἀψίκορον, ὠμόν, βάσκανον, ἀπαίδευτον, ὡς ἂν συνηρανις-
μένον ἐκ σύγκλυδος ὄχλου καὶ βιαίων φλυάρων. 'Ο δὲ          b
τούτῳ προσεταιριζόμενος ἀθλιώτερος μακρῷ.

ΣΩ.  'Οπότε οὖν, ὦ 'Αξίοχε, τὴν ἐλευθεριωτάτην
ἐπιστήμην τίθεσαι τῶν λοιπῶν ἀπευκταιοτάτην, τί τὰς
λοιπὰς ἐπιτηδεύσεις ἐννοήσομεν; οὐ φευκτάς; ἤκουσα
δέ ποτε καὶ τοῦ Προδίκου λέγοντος ὅτι ὁ θάνατος οὔτε
περὶ τοὺς ζῶντάς ἐστιν οὔτε περὶ τοὺς μετηλλαχότας.

AΞ.  Πῶς φῄς, ὦ Σώκρατες;

situations is it driven; now with joy quivering and
throbbing like fever, now with painful failure that
is worse than even a thousand deaths.  For who could          368D
be happy living for a mob if, as a plaything of the
people, he were called (like a horse) and slapped,
being driven out and hissed at, punished, killed,
pitied?[46]  Tell me, then, my political friend
Axiochus, how did Miltiades die, how Themistocles,
how Ephialtes?[47]  How the ten commanders of recent
times when I refused to ask the advice of the people?
For it did not seem honorable for me to be in command
of a mad mob.[48]  Yet on the next day Theramenes and
Callixenus,[49] having suborned the presidents of the
meeting, secured a death sentence against the ten
without a trial.  Only you and Euryptolemus defended
them,[50] though there were 30,000 citizens at the           369A
trial.

AXIOCHUS:  That's the way it is, Socrates, and
since then I have had enough of the speaker's platform--
and nothing has appeared more difficult to me than
politics.  This is obvious to those who are involved
in this business.  You speak, of course, as a distant
observer, but those of us who are going through the
experience know it more accurately.  For the common
folk, Socrates, is ungrateful, fickle, cruel, envious,
uneducated, a truly promiscuous mob come from every-
where, violent and garrulous.  And the one who plays          B
up to this rabble is the more miserable by far.

SOCRATES:  Since, then, Axiochus, you consider
the freest profession of all is to be deprecated most
of all, what shall we think of life's other pursuits?
Are they not to be avoided?[51]  I once heard even
Prodicus say that death concerns neither the living
nor those who have passed away.

AXIOCHUS:  What do you mean, Socrates?

ΣΩ. Ὅτι περὶ μὲν τοὺς ζῶντας οὐκ ἔστιν, οἱ δὲ
ἀποθανόντες οὐκ εἰσίν. Ὥστε οὔτε περὶ σὲ νῦν ἐστίν
--οὐ γὰρ τέθνηκας--οὔτε εἴ τι πάθοις, ἔσται περὶ σέ·     369c
σὺ γὰρ οὐκ ἔσῃ. Μάταιος οὖν ἡ λύπη, περὶ τοῦ μήτε
ὄντος μήτε ἐσομένου περὶ ᾽Αξίοχον ᾽Αξίοχον ὀδύρεσθαι,
καὶ ὅμοιον ὡς εἰ περὶ τῆς Σκύλλης ἢ τοῦ Κενταύρου
τις ὀδύροιτο, τῶν μήτε ὄντων περὶ σὲ μήτε ὕστερον
μετὰ τὴν τελευτὴν ἐσομένων. Τὸ γὰρ φοβερὸν τοῖς
οὖσίν ἐστι· τοῖς δ᾽ οὐκ οὖσι πῶς ἂν εἴη;

ΑΞ. Σὺ μὲν ἐκ τῆς ἐπιπολαζούσης τὰ νῦν λεσχη-      d
νείας τὰ σοφὰ ταῦτα προῄρηκας· ἐκεῖθεν γάρ ἐστιν
ἥδε ἡ φλυαρολογία πρὸς τὰ μειράκια διακεκοσμημένη·
ἐμὲ δὲ ἡ στέρησις τῶν ἀγαθῶν τοῦ ζῆν λυπεῖ, κἂν
πιθανωτέρους τούτων λόγους ἀρτικροτήσῃς, ὦ Σώκρατες.
Οὐκ ἐπαΐει γὰρ ὁ νοῦς ἀποπλανώμενος εἰς εὐεπείας
λόγων, οὐδὲ ἅπτεται ταῦτα τῆς ὁμοχροίας, ἀλλ᾽ εἰς
μὲν πομπὴν καὶ ῥημάτων ἀγλαϊσμὸν ἀνύτει, τῆς δὲ
ἀληθείας ἀποδεῖ. Τὰ δὲ παθήματα σοφισμάτων οὐκ      e
ἀνέχεται, μόνοις δὲ ἀρκεῖται τοῖς δυναμένοις
καθικέσθαι τῆς ψυχῆς.

ΣΩ. Συνάπτεις γάρ, ὦ ᾽Αξίοχε, ἀνεπιλογίστως,
τῇ στερήσει τῶν ἀγαθῶν ἀντεισάγων κακῶν αἴσθησιν,
ἐκλαθόμενος ὅτι τέθνηκας. Λυπεῖ γὰρ τὸ στερόμενον     370a
τῶν ἀγαθῶν ἡ ἀντιπάθεια τῶν κακῶν, ὁ δ᾽ οὐκ ὢν οὐδὲ
τῆς στερήσεως ἀντιλαμβάνεται. Πῶς οὖν ἐπὶ τῷ μὴ
παρέξοντι γνῶσιν τῶν λυπησόντων γένοιτ᾽ ἂν ἡ λύπη;
ἀρχὴν γάρ, ὦ ᾽Αξίοχε, μὴ συνυποτιθέμενος ἀμῶς γέ
πως μίαν αἴσθησιν, κατὰ τὸ ἀνεπιστήμον, οὐκ ἂν ποτε
πτυρείης τὸν θάνατον.

SOCRATES: That death is of no concern for the
living--as for the dead, they no longer are. Conse-      369C
quently, neither does it concern you now--for you are
not dead--nor, if you should experience something,
will it concern you, for you will not exist. Futile
is the grief to lament for Axiochus over what neither
concerns now will concern Axiochus, and it is just as
if someone were to grieve for Scylla or for the
Centaur which,[52] so far as you're concerned, neither
exist now nor will exist after your death. For what
is fearful exists only for those who are; how could
it exist for those who are not?

AXIOCHUS: These fine sayings of yours are part       D
of the current chatter of the times.[53] They are the
source of all the nonsense devised for the young.
For me, the loss of goods for living is painful, even
though you, Socrates, were to marshal more persuasive
arguments than these. For my mind pays no attention
and is not seduced by the eloquence of your words.
Such reasonings do not even touch the surface; rather
they result in a pompous parade and verbal splendor,
and fall short of the truth. Sufferings are not
content with clever arguments, but are satisfied only
with those things able to touch the soul.              E

SOCRATES: Yes, Axiochus, for you thoughtlessly
make a connection with deprivation of the goods by
introducing the awareness of evils, forgetting that
you are dead. What distresses him who is deprived     370A
of the goods is suffering of the evils in its place.
But someone who doesn't exist is unaware even of
deprivation. How, then, could there be pain for what
will provide no knowledge of the things that will
cause pain? For if at the beginning, Axiochus, you
had not unintelligently assumed in some fashion a
certain sensation for the dead,[54] you would not be

Νῦν δὲ περιτρέπεις σεαυτόν, δειματούμενος στερήσεσθαι
τῆς ψυχῆς, τῇ δὲ στερήσει περιτιθεῖς ψυχήν, καὶ
ταρβεῖς μὲν τὸ μὴ αἰσθήσεσθαι, καταλήψεσθαι δὲ οἴει
τὴν οὐκ ἐσομένην αἴσθησιν αἰσθήσει.

Πρὸς τῷ πολλοὺς καὶ καλοὺς εἶναι λόγους περὶ        370b
τῆς ἀθανασίας τῆς ψυχῆς, οὐ γὰρ δὴ θνητή γε φύσις
τοσόνδε ἂν ἤρατο μεγεθουργίας, ὥστε καταφρονῆσαι μὲν
ὑπερβαλλόντων θηρίων βίας, διαπεραιώσασθαι δὲ πελάγη,
δείμασθαι δὲ ἄστη, καταστήσασθαι δὲ πολιτείας, ἀνα-
βλέψαι δὲ εἰς τὸν οὐρανὸν καὶ ἰδεῖν περιφορὰς ἄστρων
καὶ δρόμους ἡλίου τε καὶ σελήνης, ἀνατολάς τε καὶ
δύσεις, ἐκλείψεις τε καὶ ταχείας ἀποκαταστάσεις,
ἰσημερίας τε καὶ τροπὰς διττάς, καὶ Πλειάδων χειμῶνας,    c
καὶ θέρους ἀνέμους τε καὶ καταφορὰς ὄμβρων, καὶ
πρηστήρων ἐξαισίους συρμούς, καὶ τὰ τοῦ κόσμου παθήματα παραπήξασθαι πρὸς τὸν αἰῶνα, εἰ μή τι θεῖον
ὄντως ἐνῆν πνεῦμα τῇ ψυχῇ, δι᾿ οὗ τὴν τῶν τηλικῶνδε
περίνοιαν καὶ γνῶσιν ἔσχεν. Ὥστε οὐκ εἰς θάνατον
ἀλλ᾿ εἰς ἀθανασίαν μεταβάλλεις, ὦ Ἀξίοχε, οὐδὲ
ἀφαίρεσιν ἕξεις τῶν ἀγαθῶν ἀλλ᾿ εἰλικρινεστέραν τὴν
ἀπόλαυσιν, οὐδὲ μεμειγμένας θνητῷ σώματι τὰς ἡδονὰς    d
ἀλλ᾿ ἀκράτους ἀπασῶν ἀλγηδόνων. Κεῖσε γὰρ ἀφίξῃ
μονωθεὶς ἐκ τῆσδε τῆς εἱρκτῆς, ἔνθα ἄπονα πάντα καὶ
ἀστένακτα καὶ ἀγήρατα, γαληνὸς δέ τις καὶ κακῶν
ἄπονος βίος, ἀσαλεύτῳ ἡσυχίᾳ εὐδιαζόμενος, καὶ
περιαθρῶν τὴν φύσιν, φιλοσοφῶν οὐ πρὸς ὄχλον καὶ
θέατρον ἀλλὰ πρὸς ἀμφιθαλῆ τὴν ἀλήθειαν.

ΑΞ.   Εἰς τοὐναντίον με τῷ λόγῳ περιέστακας·
οὐκέτι γάρ μοι θανάτου δέος ἔνεστιν, ἀλλ᾿ ἤδη καὶ      e
πόθος--ἵνα τι κἀγὼ μιμησάμενος τοὺς ῥήτορας περιττὸν
εἴπω--

alarmed at death.  But now you upset yourself; fearing
to be deprived of the soul, you confer on this deprivation a soul of its own.  And you dread the absence
of sensation, but you think that you will comprehend
the future absence of sensation with sensation.

In addition to the many and beautiful discourses    370B
on the immortality of the soul,[55] a mortal nature
would certainly not have arisen to such lofty attempts that it disdains the physical superiority of
wild beasts, to cross seas, to build cities, to
establish governments, to look up at the heavens and
to see the revolutions of the stars, the courses of
sun and moon, their risings and settings, their
eclipses, their swift periodic returns, the equinoxes
and the double tropics, the storms of the Pleiades,[56]
the summer winds and falls of rains and the sudden          C
fury of hurricanes, and to chart for eternity the
conditions of the universe unless there were really
some divine spirit in the soul by which it has comprehension and knowledge of such important matters.[57]
Thus, Axiochus, you change not into death, but into
immortality; neither will you have removal of the
goods, but a purer enjoyment of them, nor pleasures
mixed with the body, but undiluted by all pains.
For, released from this prison, you will come to that     D
place where all stress, mourning, and old age are
missing, and where there is a kind of life that is
tranquil and without the stress of ills.  There,
enjoying an untroubled peace and contemplating nature,
you may be a philosopher, not before a crowd and
audience, but before Truth flourishing on every side.

AXIOCHUS:  With your speech you have brought me
to the opposite point of view.  For no longer do I
have a fear of death, but now I even have a longing
for it--if I may imitate the rhetoricians and utter          E

καὶ πάλαι μετεωρολογῶ καὶ δίειμι τὸν ἀίδιον καὶ
θεῖον δρόμον, ἔκ τε τῆς ἀσθενείας ἐμαυτὸν συνείλεγμαι καὶ γέγονα καινός.

ΣΩ.  Εἰ δὲ καὶ ἕτερον βούλει λόγον, ὃν ἐμοὶ            371a
ἤγγειλε Γωβρύης, ἀνὴρ μάγος· ἔφη κατὰ τὴν Ξέρξου
διάβασιν τὸν πάππον αὐτοῦ καὶ ὁμώνυμον, πεμφθέντα
εἰς Δῆλον, ὅπως τηρήσειε τὴν νῆσον ἄσυλον ἐν ᾗ οἱ
δύο θεοὶ ἐγένοντο, ἔκ τινων χαλκέων δέλτων, ἃς ἐξ
Ὑπερβορέων ἐκόμισαν Ὦπίς τε καὶ Ἑκαέργη, ἐκμεμαθη-
κέναι μετὰ τὴν τοῦ σώματος λύσιν τὴν ψυχὴν εἰς τὸν
ἄδηλον χωρεῖν τόπον, κατὰ τὴν ὑπόγειον οἴκησιν, ἐν
ᾗ βασίλεια Πλούτωνος οὐχ ἥττω τῆς τοῦ Διὸς αὐλῆς,
ἅτε τῆς μὲν γῆς ἐχούσης τὰ μέσα τοῦ κόσμου, τοῦ δὲ      b
πόλου ὄντος σφαιροειδοῦς, οὗ τὸ μὲν ἕτερον ἡμισφαί-
ριον θεοὶ ἔλαχον οἱ οὐράνιοι, τὸ δὲ ἕτερον οἱ ὑπένερ-
θεν, οἱ μὲν ἀδελφοὶ ὄντες, οἱ δὲ ἀδελφῶν παῖδες.
Τὰ δὲ πρόπυλα τῆς εἰς Πλούτωνος ὁδοῦ σιδηροῖς
κλείθροις καὶ κλεισὶν ὠχύρωται.  Ταῦτα δὲ ἀνοίξαντα
ποταμὸς Ἀχέρων ἐκδέχεται, μεθ᾽ ὃν Κωκυτός, οὓς χρὴ
πορθμεύσαντας ἀχθῆναι ἐπὶ Μίνω καὶ Ῥαδάμανθυν, ὃ
κλῇζεται πεδίον ἀληθείας.  Ἐνταυθοῖ καθέζονται            c
δικασταὶ ἀνακρίνοντες τῶν ἀφικνουμένων ἕκαστον,
τίνα βίον βεβίωκε καὶ τίσιν ἐπιτηδεύμασιν ἐνῳκίσθη
τῷ σώματι.  Ψεύσασθαι δὲ ἀμήχανον.  Ὅσοις μὲν οὖν
ἐν τῷ ζῆν δαίμων ἀγαθὸς ἐπέπνευσεν, εἰς τὸν τῶν
εὐσεβῶν χῶρον οἰκίζονται, ἔνθα ἄφθονοι μὲν ὧραι
παγκάρπου γονῆς βρύουσι, πηγαὶ δὲ ὑδάτων καθαρῶν
ῥέουσι, παντοῖοι δὲ λειμῶνες ἄνθεσι ποικίλοις ἐαριζό-
μενοι, διατριβαὶ δὲ φιλοσόφων καὶ θέατρα ποιητῶν καὶ
κύκλιοι χοροὶ καὶ μουσικὰ ἀκούσματα,                      d

a hyperbole--and I have long talked of lofty things
and gone through the eternal and divine course,[58] and
from my weakness I have recovered, and I have become
a new person.

SOCRATES: But if you want another speech, here      371A
is what Gobryas,[59] a Persian wiseman, told me.  He
said that when Xerxes made his crossing, his grand-
father (who had the same name as himself) was sent to
Delos to keep safe as a sanctuary the island on which
two deities were born.[60] From some bronze tablets
which Opis and Hecaerge brought from the Hyperboreans,[61]
he learned that after its release from the body, the
soul went to the place unseen,[62] a dwelling beneath
the earth where Pluto's palace is not inferior to
Zeus' court, since the earth occupies the center of the      B
universe, and heaven is spherical.[63] Of this sphere,
the celestial gods obtained by lot one half, and the
other half was acquired by gods under the earth, some
of them brothers, others children of brothers.[64] The
entrance of the way to Pluto's palace is protected
with iron bolts and keys.  When the gates are opened,
the river Acheron, and then Cocytus,[65] receive those
who must be ferried across in order to be brought to
Minos and Rhadamanthys.[66] This place is called the
Plain of Truth.[67] There sit the judges interrogating      C
each of those who arrive, concerning what kind of
life he has lived and amid what pursuits while he
dwelled in his body.  It is impossible to lie.  So,
then, all whom a good daimon[68] inspired in life go to
reside in a place of the pious,[69] where the ungrudg-
ing seasons teem with fruits of every kind, where
fountains of pure water flow,[70] and where all kinds of
meadows bloom with flowers of many colors.[71] Here are
the discourses of philosophers, and performances of      D
poets, cyclic dances,[72] and concerts, well arranged

συμπόσιά τε εύμελῆ καὶ εἰλαπίναι αὐτοχορήγητοι, καὶ
ἀκήρατος ἀλυπία καὶ ἡδεῖα δίαιτα· οὔτε γὰρ χεῖμα
σφοδρὸν οὔτε θάλπος ἐγγίγνεται, ἀλλ' εὔκρατος ἀὴρ
χεῖται ἀπαλαῖς ἡλίου ἀκτῖσιν ἀνακιρνάμενος. 'Ενταῦθα
τοῖς μεμυημένοις ἐστί τις προεδρία· καὶ τὰς ὁσίους
ἀγιστείας κάκεῖσε συντελοῦσι. Πῶς οὖν οὐ σοὶ πρώτῳ
μέτεστι τῆς τιμῆς, ὄντι γεννήτῃ τῶν θεῶν; καὶ τοὺς        371e
περὶ 'Ηρακλέα τε καὶ Διόνυσον κατιόντας εἰς "Αιδου
πρότερον λόγος ἐνθάδε μυηθῆναι, καὶ τὸ θάρσος τῆς
ἐκεῖσε πορείας παρὰ τῆς 'Ελευσινίας ἐναύσασθαι.
"Οσοις δὲ τὸ ζῆν διὰ κακουργημάτων ἡλάθη, ἄγονται
πρὸς 'Ερινύων ἐπ' ἔρεβος καὶ χάος διὰ Ταρτάρου,
ἔνθα χῶρος ἀσεβῶν καὶ Δαναΐων ὑδρεῖαι ἀτελεῖς καὶ
Ταντάλου δίψος καὶ Τιτυοῦ σπλάγχνα αἰωνίως ἐσθιόμενα
καὶ γεννώμενα καὶ Σισύφου πέτρος ἀνήνυτος, οὗ τὰ
τέρματα αὖθις ἄρχει πόνων. "Ενθα θηρσὶ περιλιχμώμενοι 372
καὶ λαμπάσιν ἐπιμόνως πυρούμενοι Ποινῶν καὶ πᾶσαν
αἰκίαν αἰκιζόμενοι ἀιδίοις τιμωρίαις τρύχονται.

Ταῦτα μὲν ἐγὼ ἤκουσα παρὰ Γωβρύου, σὺ δ' ἂν
ἐπικρίνειας, 'Αξίοχε. 'Εγὼ γὰρ λόγῳ ἀνθελκόμενος
τοῦτο μόνον ἐμπέδως οἶδα, ὅτι ψυχὴ ἅπασα ἀθάνατος,
ἡ δὲ ἐκ τοῦδε τοῦ χωρίου μεταστάθεῖσα καὶ ἄλυπος.
"Ωστε ἢ κάτω ἢ ἄνω εὐδαιμονεῖν σε δεῖ, 'Αξίοχε,
βεβιωκότα εὐσεβῶς.

ΑΞ. Αἰσχύνομαί σοί τι εἰπεῖν, ὦ Σώκρατες·
τοσοῦτον γὰρ ἀποδέω τοῦ δεδοικέναι τὸν θάνατον, ὥστε
ἤδη καὶ ἔρωτα αὐτοῦ ἔχειν. Οὕτως με καὶ οὗτος ὁ
λόγος, ὡς καὶ ὁ οὐράνιος, πέπεικε, καὶ ἤδη περιφρονῶ

drinking-parties, and self-furnished feasts,[73] undiluted freedom from pain and a life of pleasure. No
fierce cold or heat is found there, but a mild climate
tempered by the sun's gentle rays is spread about.[74]
There is a certain place of honor for those who are
initiated,[75] and there they celebrate their holy
rites. How is it, then, that you do not share first
in the honor, you who are akin to the gods?[76]                       371E

And the story is that Heracles and Dionysus, in
their descent to Hades' realm, were first initiated
here and obtained courage for the journey there from
the Eleusinian goddess.[77] Those, however, who have
spent their life in crime are led by the Furies to
Erebus and Chaos through Tartarus,[78] where there is
a region of the impious, the ceaseless fetching of
water by the Danaids,[79] the thirst of Tantalus, the
entrails of Tityus eternally devoured and regenerated,
the never-resting stone of Sisyphus, whose end of
toil is again the beginning.[80] There are those who        372
are being licked clean by wild beasts, set persis-
tently on fire by the torches of the Avengers,[81]
and who, tortured with every kind of torture, are
consumed by everlasting punishments.

These things I heard from Gobyras; but you must
decide for yourself, Axiochus. For I, drawn by
reason, know only this for a certainty: that every
soul is immortal, and that when removed from this
place, it is also free from pain. Consequently,
either below or above, you must be happy, Axiochus,
if you have lived piously.[82]

AXIOCHUS: I am ashamed to say anything to you,
Socrates. For I am so far from fearing death that I
now feel love toward it.[83] In such a way has this
discourse, as well as the one about the heavens,
convinced me. Now I despise life, since I'm ready

τοῦ ζῆν, ἄτε εἰς ἀμείνω οἶκον μεταστησόμενος. Νυνὶ
δὲ ἠρέμα κατ' ἐμαυτὸν ἀναριθμήσομαι τὰ λεχθέντα.
Ἐκ μεσημβρίας δὲ παρέσῃ μοι, ὦ Σώκρατες.

ΣΩ. Ποιήσω ὡς λέγεις, κἀγὼ δὲ ἐπάνειμι ἐς
Κυνόσαργες, ἐς περίπατον, ὁπόθεν δεῦρο μετεκλήθην.

to move to a better home.   And now quietly, by myself,
I'll go over what has been said.   But after midday,
be with me, Socrates.

   SOCRATES:   I will do as you ask; and I'll now
return to the Cynosarges, to my walk, from which I
was summoned here.

## TRANSLATION

[1]The dialogue's beginning and the mention of hurrying along the wall (364D) is similar to the beginnings of the *Lysis* 203A: "I was going from the Academy straight to the Lyceum, by the road outside the wall..."; and of the *Smp.* 172A: "Lately I happened to be going to town from my house in Phalerum, when one of my acquaintances caught sight of me from behind and called me from some way off...."
The geographical setting of the *Axiochus* is southeast Athens in the area of the Olympeion (on which see R. E. Wyncherley, *The Stones of Athens* [Princeton: Princeton University, 1978] 155-74). Socrates has presumably left the city through the Diomeian gates for the Cynosarges which lay somewhere before them (W. Judeich, *Topographie von Athen* [2nd ed.; Munich: Beck, 1931] 141 n. 2). Located near the Ilisus, the famous river bordering southern Athens, the Cynosarges was one of the famous gymnasia of the city. It was sacred to Heracles, and used by young men of doubtful citizenship. Antisthenes the Cynic taught there in the fourth century B.C. (D.L. 6.1,13), and later in the third century, Ariston of Chios, who founded a sect, a branch of Stoicism returning to Cynic views (see Wyncherley, *Stones of Athens*, 229-31 and Judeich, *Topographie*, 422-24).
Near the Ilisus, Socrates is shouted after by Cleinias and his friends who are running to the Callirrhoe, a spring in the bed of the river (on the confusion about this spring and the Enneacrounos near the Odeion, see Judeich, *Topographie*, 193-202, and Wyncherley, *Stones of Athens*, 248-50). They all meet, and go to the Itonian gates (365A; which led southward and were probably named after Athena Itonia; see Judeich, *Topographie*, 141 n. 2) near which Axiochus lived within the city close to the monument (*stēlē*) of Antiope the Amazon (see Judeich, *Topographie*, 386).

[2]Axiochus, an Athenian, was son of Alcibiades the elder, and uncle of the famous Alcibiades (*Euthyphr.* 275A). Together with his nephew, he was charged with impiety and went into exile (Andoc. I.16). Cleinias, son of Axiochus, was the lover of Charmides and of Critobulus (see Xen. *Smp.* 4.12ff. 25; *Mem.* 1.3,8,10; cf. *Euthyphr.* 271B, 273A, 274B). Charmides was the nephew of the oligarch Critias, uncle of Plato, and a very handsome youth (*Chm.* 154 and 155A). He belonged to Socrates' circle and is often mentioned as a loyal follower (*Prt.* 315A; *Thg.* 128D, *Smp.* 222B). Socrates encouraged him to pursue a political life (Xen. *Mem.* 3.7), and together with Critias, he was leader of the oligarchic revolution of 404. In 403 he fell with Critias against the democrats led by Thrasybulus (Xen. *HG*

53

2.4,19).  Damon, tutor of Pericles, was famous for his
metrical and musical skills; see Diels-Kranz, *Die Fragmente der Vorsokratiker*, Vol. 1 (8th ed.; Berlin, 1956)
381-84.  For a recent assessment of his musical doctrines
and importance in Greek education, see C. Lord ("On Damon
and Music Education," *Hermes* 106 [1978] 33-43).

[3]A strange construction which does not mean "the
wisdom of which you boast," for Socrates himself made no
claim to wisdom, and always professed to be an inquirer
(see 366B-C).  The phrase means something like the "wisdom
attributed to you" or your "much talked-about (by others)
wisdom."  A. Brinkmann ("Beiträge zur Kritik und Erklärung
des Dialogs *Axiochos*," *Rheinisches Museum* 51 [1896] 453)
noted that a peculiarity of the *Axiochus* is the use of πρός
with the genitive after a passive instead of ὑπό (cf. 365B,
371E).

[4]"By a sudden illness": the expression is unusual.
I have followed Souilhé who agrees with Fischer (cited by
him, *Axiochos*, 137f.) that ὥρα refers not so much to a
period of time, but to an event or happening such that
someone is suddenly and unexpectedly (αἰφνίδιος) overcome
by it, and thus deprived of his powers.  Souilhé translates
ἕκ τινος ὥρας simply as "...frappé subitement d'une faib-
lesse" ("...struck suddenly by a weakness").  There is,
however, merit to Hermann's emendation ὡρακίας which he
derived from ὡρακιᾶν ("to faint") and took to mean "a swoon"
or "fainting spell."  Hence, Feddersen's "infolge einer
plötzlichen Ohnmacht."  Without αἰφνιδίου, the sense would
be "for some time," and E. O'Neil suggested to me in a
letter the possibility that some scribe became confused and
wrote a gloss which crept into the text.  This is possible.
So also is Hermann's emendation, though the word ὡρακία is
nowhere attested.

[5]"Scared of death": the verb μορμολύττομαι seldom
seems to mean "fear" or "be afraid of."  Often found in the
middle voice, it has the sense "to frighten or scare in the
manner of the bugbear (Mormo)."  Afraid of death, Axiochus'
contemporaries perhaps made fun of it by comparing it to
the Mormo, a figure of folktale and a bogey used to
frighten children (also in an exclamatory sense, "boo,
(Mormo) the horse bites," Theoc. 15.40); see *LSJ*, s.v.
See also J. Tambornino, *PW* 16 (1935) cols. 309-11, and
E. Rohde, *Psyche* (trans. W. B. Hillis; London: Routledge
& Kegan Paul, 1950) note on 592.  Chevalier (*Etude critique*, 45) noted that ἐκφοβεῖν, which the Scholiast gives
as a synonym of μορμολύττειν or μορμολυξάσθαι, is used in
the passive with the accusative of the person one fears,
Soph. *El.* 276.
There seems to be a slight inconsistency in Cleinias'
remarks because of "gently."  Hermann bracketed πρᾴως; I
have retained it.

<sup>6</sup>Cf. εἰς τὸ χρεὼν ἀπιέναι, 365B. A similar use of
τὸ χρεών (lit. "what is necessary" or "fate") in the sense
of death occurs often in the Cynic-Stoic tradition (see
Lucian *Herm*. 6, *D. Mort*. 27.9) where one should meet it
without blame of reproach (ἀμέμπτως, without μεμψιμοιρία,
vel sim.). Ἀστενακτί, lit. "without groaning" (cf. 370D,
ἀστένακτα): both adverb and adjective are found in Plutarch, *Cons. ad. Apoll*. 107A: ὃ [χρέος] εὐκόλως καταβλη-
τέον ἀστενάκτως or 305D, *Paral. Graec.*: ...ἀστενάκτως
ὑπομείνας τὴν ἀνάγκην.

<sup>7</sup>"That this can be dealt with in a reverent way":
a somewhat strange construction in which ἵνα is displaced.
Chevalier (*Etude critique*, 45) remarked that it is an "in-
frequent inversion, rather poetic, and which appears to be
a latinism," cf. Cic. *Div*. I.40: *deus ut haberetur*.
Εὐσεβεῖν in the passive sense of "to be accomplished
piously" presumably refers to Axiochus' impending death
which his son wants accomplished or handled in a reverent
way without complaint not only on Axiochus' part, but also
on his own part and that of the rest of the family and
friends.

<sup>8</sup>"...recovered from his ailments": in a critique of
my initial translation, R. Kotansky noted that ἀφή can mean
"infection" or "disease" (see *LSJ*, s.v. [8]). And at 370E
Axiochus says "I have recovered (συνείλεγμαι, the same verb
as here) from my weakness." Often ἀφή refers to the sense
of touch or the grip in wrestling (*LSJ*, s.v. [2] and [4]),
but such a meaning seems doubtful here. Souilhé argued
(*Axiochus*, 138f.) that τὰς ἀφάς can be given a broader
meaning, a part for the whole, and so touch for all the
senses. But "recovered his senses" would suggest Axiochus
is now strong in spirit, a notion contradicted by the further description of Axiochus as strong in body, but "weak
in spirit." Another possibility is that Axiochus has re-
gained use of his limbs or joints (on the derivation of
ἀφή from ἅπτω, see H. Frisk, *Griechisches Etymologisches
Wörterbuch* [Heidelberg, 1960] s.v.).

<sup>9</sup>"Beating of hands": an interesting cultural phe-
nomenon as a sign of despair (cf. the Latin phrase *complo-
sis manibus*). The expression "to beat the hands" is found
in Attic authors (see *LSJ*, s.v. κροτέω; cf. 368D), but
κρότησις is rare, and the plural use, as here, is extraordinary (Chevalier, *Etude critique*, 47).

<sup>10</sup>"One who listens to rational arguments": in *LSJ* the
expression is rendered "student of philosophy," and by
Souilhé as "one who receives good lessons." Another possibility suggested by Edward O'Neil in a critique of my
translation is "one who listens to reason" or "rational
arguments"). *Logos* has a number of meanings in Greek, and
in the present context where the plural is used, Socrates
clearly appeals to Axiochus' rational side.

[11]The notion of life as a brief stay in a foreign
land is common in antiquity: cf. M. Ant. 2.17, "life is...
a sojourning (ἐπιδημία) in a foreign country"; but παρεπιδημία is rarely used in its present metaphorical sense
(cf. Hipparch., ap. Stob. 4.44.81), and appears to be late
(see Chevalier, *Etude critique*, 47); cf. biblical usage:
Gen 23:4; Ps 39:12; Heb 11:13; 1 Pet 1:1, 2:11. The idea
that life is a sojourn may be Orphic in origin (A. Dieterich, *Nekyia* [3rd ed.; Stuttgart: B. G. Teubner, 1969]
88).

[12]"So unwilling to be torn from life": it is a commonplace that one should follow death voluntarily, but the
expression δυσαποσπάστως ἔχειν is found only here and in
Aesop, *Fab.* 84, Diod. Sic. 20.51; Iamb. *Vita Pyth.* 58;
John Chrysostom, 7.408 (*P.G.*, vol. 57,414).

[13]Here and later (369D, 370A, 370C) there are references to τὰ ἀγαθά, that is, not "good" as opposed to evil,
but "the goods." See E. O'Neil's *Teles (The Cynic Teacher)*
(Missoula: Scholars Press, 1977) (I.17ff [3H-4H] and n. 3,
p. 73, and III.9-36 [22H-23H]), where Teles quotes Stilpon,
and the "goods" are divided into three categories: "goods"
of the soul, "goods" of the body, and external "goods."

[14]"Because of your thoughtlessness, you uncritically
connect sensation with absence of sensation...such as you
had before birth": Immisch (*Philologische Studien*, 26)
followed Winckelmann in considering "because of your
thoughtlessness" a gloss; cf. 369E where the same intro-
ductory phrase, "you uncritically connect..." (συνάπτεις
...ἀνεπιλογίστως), occurs without "because of your thoughtlessness." Nonetheless, the passage is probably Epicurean
in sentiment, including some vocabulary: ἀνεπιστασία
("thoughtlessness") is in Phld., *Ir.* p. 33 Wilke; ἀνεπι-
λόγιστος ("uncritically") is a hapax, but see Epicur. *Sent.
Vat.* 63 and Diogenian. Epicur. 3.25; on ἀναισθησία and
death as a lack of sensation, see Epicurus, ap. D.L. 10.81.
The belief that death is a state or condition like that
before birth was a fairly common one (e.g. *C.I.L.* [IX.
4840]: "once we were not--then we were born--and now we
rest..." (*olim non fuimus, nati sumus unde quieti nunc
sumus...*) and is also found in the Epicurean Lucretius
3.830f. (cf. this and the *Axiochus* passage with Epicurus,
D.L. 10.124-127, and Cicero, *Tusc.* I.38,91).

[15]Draco was a famous Athenian legislator of the
seventh century B.C. noted for the severity of his code--
hence, our word "draconian." Cleisthenes was an early
sixth-century reformer of Athens' political constitution.

[16]"The corpse...is not the human person. For we are soul...": the thought is like that of *Alc.* I.130C: "since neither the body nor the combination of the two is a human person, it follows either that the human person is nothing at all, or if something, the human person is nothing other than soul" (...μηδὲν ἄλλο τὸν ἄνθρωπον...ἢ ψυχήν); cf. the conclusion "the soul is the human person" (ἡ ψυχή ἐστιν ἄνθρωπος). On the *Alcibiades* passage, see H. D. Betz, "The Delphic Maxim ΓΝΩΘΙ ΣΑΥΤΟΝ in Hermetic Interpretation," *HTR* 63 (1970) 465-84, esp. 471ff., and Guthrie, *History* 3/2. 150ff., and 5.394. A turning point is here reached in the *Axiochus* as Socrates shifts his argument from popular Epicureanism to serious Platonism. For contrasting Epicurean views on the soul, see Rist, *Epicurus*, 74ff. See also A. Dihle, ψυχή, *TDNT* 9.904ff.

[17]The view of the body as a prison is Platonic (see *Cra.* 400C, *Phd.* 62B, 82E, and *Grg.* 493), and probably Orphic in origin; see Guthrie, *History*, 4.339 nn. 1 and 2, and 5.395 n. 1.

[18]On the "tent" (σκῆνος) as a metaphor for the human body, a famous notion in antiquity, see W. Michaelis, *TDNT* 9, s.v. σκῆνος. Cf. Plato, *Phd.* 81C; Philo, *Quaest. in Gen.* 1.28; *PGM* I.319; 4.448, 1951, 1970, 2141; *Corp. Herm.* V; Clem. Al. *Strom.* V.94,3 (see also Lampe, *Patristic Greek Lexicon*, s.v.).

[19]The idea that the soul is spread throughout the body's pores, and that sensation occurs through these, is Epicurean; see Rist, *Epicurus*, 80ff. On "pores" in Epicurus, see Index in Arrighetti, *Epicuro: Opere* (= *Classici della Filosofia*, IV) (Turin: G. Einaudi, 1960) 651 s.v. πόρος.

[20]The belief that the aither, the pure, fiery substance above the earth's air and originally home of the gods, is the place of the souls of the dead appears in the fifth century, e.g. *C.I.A.* 1.442, an epigram on fallen of Potidaea (432 B.C.): "the aither has received their souls"; cf. Eur. *El.* 59; *Hel.* 1014-16. The notion became important among the Stoics and the Romans. See J. H. Waszink, "Aether," *RAC* 1 (1950) 150-58, esp. 154-55. See also Dillon, *Middle Platonists*, 49, 169, 170, 286, 315, and Guthrie, *Socrates*, 156f. Traces of the idea are found in Plato *R.* 10.616B-C, but it is in the pseudo-Platonic *Epinomis* that the doctrine of aither is prominent. Reading doctrines into the *Timaeus*, the author introduced five simple bodies of which aither was one. The other four are earth, air, fire, and water. The *daimones* are placed in the region of aither. On this conception in the *Epinomis*,

see L. Tarán, *Academica: Plato Philip of Opus and the
Pseudo-Platonic Epinomis* (Philadelphia: American Philosophical Society, 1975) 36ff. and Guthrie, *History*, 5.386
and 395 n. 1.

[21]"The release from this life is a change...to a
good": cf. Socrates' closing remarks in the *Ap.* 40C-D;
death "is, according to things said, a change (μεταβολή)
and migration (μετοίκησις) of the soul from this to
another place," and "if this is true, what greater good
could there be...?" See also Guthrie, *Socrates* (147ff.,
esp. 158ff.) for an assessment of Socrates' views on the
soul as found in Plato.

[22]"You are a thinker": Socrates is derisively called
a φροντιστής by Ar. *Nu.* 266; cf. Plato *Ap.* 18B; see *LSJ*,
s.v.

[23]"I often wish I knew...": Socrates' famous statement
of his ignorance (see Guthrie, *Socrates*, 122ff.); τοσοῦτον
is a late and unusual construction for τοσόσδε (cf. 372B):
"so far am I from (knowing)...." The contrast between
"ordinary matters" (τὰ κοινά) and "extraordinary matters"
(τὰ περιττά, cf. Souilhé's "idées sublimes") is not wholly
clear. Τὰ κοινά perhaps refers to civic, "common" affairs
of mortals (cf. *Hp. Ma.* 282B, τὰ κοινὰ πράττειν), for according to Xenophon (*Mem.* 1.1,10), Socrates frequented
public places, talked with anyone about human affairs, but
avoided speculation on abstruse subjects such as the nature
of the cosmos. Human affairs should not be neglected at
the expense of the divine. The περιττά would thus seem to
be subtle, refined matters, perhaps pertaining to metaphysical speculation.

[24]Prodicus of Ceos, a famous Sophist, is mentioned
several times in Plato as Socrates' teacher or friend (see
Guthrie, *History* 3/1. 222-23 and 275f.). That Prodicus
charged a fee for his instruction on the "correctness" of
names is attested at *Cra.* 384B, and there seems to have
been a joke about the difference between his one-drachma
lecture and his fifty-drachma lecture (ibid., 275 and 42
n. 1). His works are lost except possibly for an *epideixis*
or speech before a popular audience on Heracles and virtue
(Xen. *Mem.* 2.1,21-34; see Guthrie, *History* 3/1. 277f.). It
is a question how much, if any, of the *epideixis* in the
*Axiochus* can be attributed to him. Chevalier remarks with
some justice (*Etude critique*, 72-73) that Prodicus is only
a figurehead ("préte-nom") whom the author of the *Axiochus*
has used to express ideas that could not be attributed to
Socrates. In a letter to me, Edward O'Neil pointed out
that what Chevalier says about Prodicus is also in keeping
with the rule for χρεία as set forth in the Greek

grammarians, e.g. Hermogenes. In fact, the use of some
appropriate character in such χρεῖαι is what sets them
apart from γνῶμαι which are anonymous. Thus, there is
possibly a Cynic influence on pseudo-Plato.

[25]Epicharmus: a comic poet of the sixth century, known
for expressing contemporary philosophical ideas in his
works. The saying in the *Axiochus* is in Diels-Kranz, *Die
Fragmente der Vorsokratiker*, B 30 (1.203); cf. Sen. *Apocol.*
9 and Petr. *Sat.*, 45: *manus manum lavat* ("a hand washes a
hand").

[26]Callias was a wealthy Athenian and patron of the
Sophists. His house is the setting for Xenophon's *Sympos-
ium* and Plato's *Protagoras*. See Guthrie, *Sophists*, 41 and
306.

[27]The soul's longing for death is a famous Socratic
notion; see Guthrie, *Socrates*, 164.

[28]The great similarity between 366D-367B and *Teles* V
("On Pleasure Not Being the Goal of Life") was noted on pp.
16f. of my introduction. See also O'Neil's notes to the
fragment in his *Teles* (p. 91). There are also similarities
between the *Axiochus* passage, and the pseudo-Platonic *Epinomis* (973D-974A): "from the beginning existence is difficult for every live creature...being born and further, being reared and educated...swiftly old age is upon us."
Tarán thus speculates that in writing a "Platonic" dialogue, the author of the *Axiochus* would have looked for a
source and found one in the *Epinomis* passage (*Academica*,
156 n. 669, and 210). Whether the *Axiochus* passage is influenced by Teles or by the *Epinomis*, there is evidence
for a date after the fourth-third centuries B.C.

[29]Though the ensuing account of an Athenian youth's
education is loosely given, the report that he began formal
study at the age of seven is supported by Aristotle (*Pol.*
1336a 41ff.) who writes that the young received instruction
at home until seven years of age (see W. L. Newman, *Politics of Aristotle* [Oxford, 1902] 3.488-89; cf. Plato, *Lg.*
794C). On the tutors (παιδαγωγοί) and elementary school
teachers (γραμματισταί), see H. Marrou, *Histoire de l'édu-
cation dans l'antiquité* (Paris, 1948) 202f. See also E.
Schuppe, *PW* 18.1 (1942) s.v. "paidagogos," cols. 2375-85;
on the physical trainers (παιδοτρίβαι), see J. Jüthner,
*PW* 18.1 (1942) s.v. "paidotribes," cols. 2389-96, esp.
2394. There Jüthner, in reference to the *Axiochus*, notes
that the physical trainers often treated their charges
harshly (see also Marrou, *Histoire*, 221f. on education and
chastisement).

[30]On "language teachers" (κριτικοί), see Gudeman (*PW*
11 (1922) s.v. κριτικός, cols. 1912-15), who notes that,
although the terms κριτικός and γραμματικός were synony-
mous in the post-Alexandrian period (κριτικός appears to
have been an earlier technical term), the latter term became prevalent (col. 1913). On geometry instruction, see
H. Marrou, *Histoire*, 245ff. On the military instruction,
see E. Lammert and F. Lammert, *PW* 11 (1922) s.v. "Kriegs-
kunst," cols. 1827-58; presumably the τακτικοί gave instruction in the movements and use of weapons of the
hoplites.

[31]The director (κοσμητής) of the Ephebes was an offi-
cial title at Athens. He is mentioned only twice in literary sources, here and in Stob. *Flor.* III.235, 72, but
the term appears often in inscriptions from the fourth
century B.C. until the third century A.D. See F. Preis-
igke, *PW* 11 (1922) s.v. "κοσμητής," cols. 1490-95. On the
ephebes, see Marrou, *Histoire*, 152ff., and M. P. Nilsson,
*Die hellenistische Schule* (Munich, 1955) 17ff. Among the
duties of the director was to provide the ephebes with oil
for rubdowns and to teach them practice in arms and horse-
back riding.

[32]The Lyceum was the shrine of Apollo Lyceius ("wolf-
god") where Aristotle set up his school, on which see J. P.
Lynch (*Aristotle's School* [Berkeley, 1972]); the Academy
was a shrine sacred to Academus or Hecademus, but the word
was also used of the gymnasium there, Plato's school, and
of the district. On both gymnasia and schools, see Wyncherley, *Stones of Athens*, 219-29.

[33]On the Areopagus (a famous hill west of the Acropolis) on which met the oldest council in Athens having
special jurisdiction in homicide cases, see T. Thalheim,
*PW* 2 (1896) s.v. "Areios pagos," cols. 627-33. On its
later importance, see Plu. *Cic.* 24 and Acts 17:19.

[34]"Perishable" (δυσαλθές) seems almost a synonym for
"mortal" (ἐπίκηρον). Literally the phrase might be rendered "subject to death and deadly"; cf. Phld. *Mort.* 38,
τὸ θνητὸν καὶ ἐπίκηρον.

[35]Cf. Cic. *Tusc.* I.39,93: Nature "has granted life
like a loan, without fixing any day for repayment"
(...*dedit usuram vitae tamquam pecuniae nulla prestituta
die*).

[36]On this phrase, lit. "a second time the aged become
children," the Scholiast quotes a line of the *Delians* by
the comic poet Cratinus: "the saying then was true: that a
second time the old man is a child: (δὶς παῖς...ὁ γέρων);
cf. Plato, *Lg.* 646A: "Not only then, so it seems, does the

old man become a child a second time (ὁ γέρων δὶς παῖς
γίνεται), but even the drunk"; Ar. *Nu.* 1417; and see also
*Teles* V.32-33 where the aged person "submits to being
waited on like a child," and *Epin.* 974A 7 (and Tarán's
comment, *Academica*, 212). The saying was obviously a
commonplace in antiquity.

[37]Perhaps a reworking of Menander, Frag. 125: "he
whom the gods love dies young" (ὃν οἱ θεοὶ φιλοῦσιν ἀπο-
θνῄσκει νέος). Quoted also by Plutarch, *Cons. ad Apoll.*
119E. If the sentence is a reworking of Menander, it is
still another indication that the *Axiochus* is late; see
notes 38 and 39 following.

[38]The brothers or half-brothers Agamedes and Trophonius were legendary heroes of architecture; see O. Kern,
*PW* 1 (1894) s.v. "Agamedes," cols. 719-21, and H. G. Radke,
*PW* 7.1, 2nd series (1939) s.v. "Trophonios," cols. 678-95,
esp. 694. A very similar story about their easeful death
is found in Cic. *Tusc.* I.47,114, and Plutarch, *Cons. ad
Apoll.* 109A-B (cf. Pindar, Frag. 2).

[39]The sons were Biton and Cleobis, and their mother
Cydippe. The earliest version of the famous sons is in
Herodotus I,31; see K. K. Müller, *PW* 3 (1899) s.v. "Biton,"
cols. 544-46. In Plutarch's *Cons. ad Apoll.* 108F, the
story of Biton and Cleobis appears *before* that of Agamedes
and Trophonius. The author of the *Axiochus* has thus re-
versed them, but the occurrence of both stories in the
*Cons. ad Apoll.* and in the *Axiochus* is an indication that
the latter work belongs to the "consolation" tradition.
Indeed, the stories as well as the catena of quotations
following from 367D-368A is reminiscent of Plutarch's
*Cons. ad Apoll.*, a work often criticized for excessive
quotation. But this seems to be a regular feature of
consolations.

[40]This and the following quotation are from Homer,
*Il.* 24.525-26 and *Il.* 17.446-47 respectively. R. Lattimore's translations are used for these verses.

[41]Amphiaraus was one of the Seven against Thebes,
swallowed alive by a cleft in the earth made by Zeus'
thunderbolt as he was driven off from the city (see H. J.
Rose, *A Handbook of Greek Mythology* [New York, 1959]
190ff.). The quotation following is from *Od.* 15.245-46
(R. Lattimore's translation) on which a Scholiast aptly
quotes Menander: "he whom the gods love, dies young."

[42]This line is from Euripides' lost *Cresphontes*, Frag.
452 (Dindorf). Cicero quotes the fragment in Latin at
*Tusc.* I.48,115, adding that a similar thought is in
Crantor's *Consolation*.

[43]The passage seems a bit odd because of the genitive
plural participles. They are probably best understood as
dependent ("subjective") genitives (on which see, for example, H. W. Smyth, *Greek Grammar* [Cambridge, MA, 1972]
319). They follow χειρωνατικὰς...καὶ βαναύσους (a two-
termination adjective) which modify τέχνας understood.
Thus, χειρωνατικὰς...καὶ βαναύσους (sc. τέχνας) of those
laboring etc. Cf. τέχναις τινός, Pi. *O.* 9.52, "by his
arts" (or by his agency). By the exercise of their
skills, craftsmen labor from night to night...deplore
themselves (αὐτῶν, or "their lives," cf. 367D, κατοδύρονται
τὸ ζῆν) etc. Except for Stobaeus, the mss. have accusative plurals πονομένους instead of πονουμένων, ποριζομέ-
νους instead of ποριζομένων which would be attractive to
adopt if χειρωνατικὰς...βαναύσους were not substantival
adjectives but rather independent nouns.

[44]Bias was always included among the seven sages of
Greece; see B. Snell, *Leben und Meinungen der Sieben
Weisen* [4th ed.; Munich, 1971]). Some sayings attributed
to him were probably by Bion the Cynic; see Souilhé,
*Axiochus*, 143 n. 3, and Crusius, *PW* 3 (1899) s.v. "Bias,"
cols. 383-89, esp. 389.

[45]Souilhé assumes δῆλον ("obviously") is spoken by
Socrates. The ἀλλά that follows, however, suggests that a
different person is speaking. Hence, the "obviously" is
best taken as a remark by Axiochus. Socrates' subsequent
remarks on farming are reminiscent of Menander's *Dyskolos*,
e.g. 604f.: the Attic farmer takes "nothing good" from his
labors.

[46]The remarks about politics are not complimentary.
In particular, the verbs ποππυσθείη καὶ κροτηθείη cannot
easily be rendered, as does Souilhé, by "des flatteries et
des applaudissements." As the Scholiast notes, ποππυσθείη
is here used metaphorically. It's a term employed in training horses (see *LSJ*, s.v.), thus the politician is summoned, like a horse, with a clucking sound or smacking of
the lips. κροτέω in the passive "to be beaten" or "struck"
seems to mean here "slapped" as one slaps a horse. "Pitied"
(ἐλεούμενον) after "killed" seems almost anticlimatic and
is omitted by Stobaeus.

[47]Miltiades, hero of Marathon, having led an unsuccess-
ful campaign against Paros, was fined and died soon after
in 489 B.C.; Themistocles, a famous Athenian statesman was,
for alleged treason, ostracized in 470 B.C. and died in
exile in 462; Ephialtes, friend of Pericles, worked to les-
sen the powers of the Areopagus about 462 B.C. and was
killed by a hired assassin.

[48]Socrates refers to the trial of ten naval commanders who, after the battle of Arginusae in 406 B.C., were charged with failure to rescue crewmen of damaged ships and to retrieve the corpses of those slain in battle. Their investigation was conducted illegally, and Socrates, chairman of the committee at which the issue was discussed, refused to have it put before the Assembly. See Plato, *Ap*. 32A-C and Xenophon, *HG* I.7,12-15 and *Mem*. 1.1,18 and 4.4,2, and Guthrie, *Socrates*, 59f.

[49]Theramenes, an Athenian politician, who was ordered to help the wrecked ships, laid blame on the ten commanders thus escaping punishment; Callixenus proposed having the Assembly of the citizens decide the commanders' guilt or innocence by a secret vote, thus accusing them *en bloc*.

[50]Euryptolemus, cousin of Alcibiades, objected to Callixenus' proposal but was induced, by threat of including him in the accusation, to withdraw his objection.

[51]Since the transition from this question to Socrates' following mention of Prodicus' belief seems abrupt, Buresch assumed a lacuna after οὐ φευκτάς. He was rightly refuted by Feddersen (*Über den Axiochus*, 10-11) who noted Socrates has already discussed life's other pursuits (368A-C) and need not repeat his views. If life's pursuits are to be shunned, death can be no evil as it frees us from them. Prodicus' belief that death concerns neither the living nor the dead is quite appropriately mentioned at this point.

[52]Feddersen (*Über den Axiochus*, 5) believed the author of the *Axiochus* was thinking of the famous centaur, Cheiron, and thus proposed ἢ Χείρωνος τοῦ κενταύρου. But his proposed reading is unnecessary since "the centaur" probably stands for any member of the class of chimerical beings; see Souilhé, *Axiochus*, 145.

[53]The sentiments expressed by Socrates at 369B-C are clearly Epicurean. "Chatter" (λεσχηνεία) is a hapax, derived from originally meaning "couch"; hence, lounging place of idlers or beggars; see *LSJ*, s.v.

[54]Literally, "had you not unintelligently assumed...a certain sensation" (μίαν αἴσθησιν). The Greek seems odd, but εἷς can be used indefinitely (see *LSJ*, s.v. 3), and I have supplied "for the dead" in an attempt to make the argument clearer. The following remarks of Socrates are an elaboration of Axiochus' unintelligent (ignorant?) assumption: Axiochus thinks that when dead he will still have sensation enabling him to perceive he has no sensation!

[55]Several scholars (e.g. Buresch, *Consolationum a
Graecis Romanisque scriptarum historia critica* [= *Leipziger
Studien zur Klassischen Philologie* 9/1] [Leipzig: S. Hirzel,
1886] 14, and Immisch, *Philologische Studien*, 39) believed
that before this sentence and after αἰσθήσει in the preceding sentence there is a lacuna. Otherwise, the transition πρὸς τῷ πολλοὺς καὶ καλοὺς κτλ. ("moreover, or in
addition to the many etc.") cannot be explained. But as
Brinkmann ("Beiträge," 447) and Souilhé (*Axiochus*, 146)
noted, the hypothesis of a lacuna is superfluous. The
argument which follows the supposed lacuna is, in fact, a
discourse (λόγος) on immortality as are the preceding
discourses, and the phrase πρὸς τῷ... should be taken to
mean "in addition to the many beautiful discourses on the
soul's immortality,..." On the sense of πρὸς τῷ, cf.
Plato, *Phd.* 106C and *Lg.* 764A.

[56]I follow Souilhé's text, but the passage seems odd
as it stands, and various suggestions have been made.
Immisch and others removed "risings and settings" (ἀνατολάς
τε καὶ δύσεις) from their present position and placed them
after "Pleiades." Various proposals have been made about
χειμῶνας καὶ θέρους; perhaps Brinkmann ("Beiträge," 447)
was correct in suggesting the "Pleiades" should be omitted
as a gloss made by a reader who missed a reference to the
famous constellation.

[57]A passage from Philo (*Quod. det. potiori insid.* 87-
90) is a striking parallel to this passage beginning at
370B: "For how could a mortal nature at one and the same
time have stayed home and been abroad...or have sailed
around at sea and traversed earth to its farthest bounds,
or have grasped laws and customs....have also apprehended
things on high, air and its changes...and all that is
brought about by the seasons of the years...examine the
condition and movement of the heavenly bodies....devise
arts and sciences....How, then, was it likely that the mind
of man being so small, contained in such small bulks as a
brain or a heart, should have room for all the vastness of
sky and universe, had it not been an inseparable portion
of that divine and blessed soul" (εἰ μὴ τῆς θείας καὶ
εὐδαίμονος ψυχῆς ἐκείνης ἀπόσπασμα ἦν οὐ διαιρετόν; Colson
and Whitaker trans., Philo, *LCL* 2 (1958). Socrates' speech
also seems somewhat reminiscent of *Epin.* 983B: a thing can
never become a spirit or alive (ἔμψυχον) except by god.
Cf. also Cic. *Tusc.* I.63: *Ne in sphaera quidem eosdem motus
Archimedes sine divino ingenio potuisset imitari*: "neither
could Archimedes have reproduced the same motions upon a
globe without divine genius"; and Sen. *Cons. Helv.* 20 for
yet another parallel to the passage.

[58]Axiochus' remark seems odd. Brinkmann noted that
μετεωρολογῶ ("I talk of lofty things"?) does not harmonize
with δίειμι ("I go through") and Axiochus has, in any
case, been silent for some time ("Beiträge," 454). He
thus proposed μετεωροπολῶ ("I busy myself with high
things"). This is a possibility, but part of the problem
rests with καὶ πάλαι. Hermann proposed κάμπαλιν which
means something like "and on the contrary" or indicates
that Axiochus has been brought to the "opposite opinion."
But this also does not help much. Now πάλαι is used with
a present to denote an act which began in the past and
lasted to the present; thus "I have long talked of lofty
things." Combined with the fact that Axiochus has recovered from his weakness (συνείλεγμαι), his remarks could
be understood as referring to his condition *before* his
illness. Early in the work (364B-C and 365A-B) we learned
that Axiochus scorned those who were afraid of death,
praised manly virtues, and listened to rational arguments.
He has now recovered something of his old self and in the
process has become "a new person." Perhaps as a result of
Socrates' consolation he has come to a fuller realization
or better understanding of what he professed in the past.
     Such an explanation, however, does not do full jus-
tice to δίειμι κτλ. Presumably the δρόμος refers to the
course of the heavenly bodies; see e.g. Dio Chrys. 19(36).
42; M. Ant. 7.47; *PGM* XII.251 and XIII.575; *Dg.* 7:2. But
how has Axiochus traveled this course?
     Now Brinkmann claimed that Axiochus' remark that he
is imitating the rhetoricians refers to what follows:
μετεωρολογῶ καὶ δίειμι κτλ. Cf. Heidel (*Pseudo-Platonica*,
17-18) who took this sentence as evidence of padding and
that the author was misled by Stoic interest in astronomy
and meterology. Possibly, then, it is a mistake to see
any real connection of the phrase with Axiochus' own situation or the previous development of the dialogue. It is a
mere rhetorical flourish devoid of any real significance.
Or is it perhaps even a quotation from an unknown source?
     Yet another possibility is that something has fallen
from the text preceding the line. Whatever the case, the
sentence remains puzzling.

[59]Gobryas is mentioned by Hdt. 7.72. He was one of
the leaders of Xerxes' army. But that he made a trip to
Delos is stated only in the *Axiochus*, and the existence of
a "wiseman" (possibly "Magian" or member of a Median tribe;
see *LSJ*, s.v. Μάγος) by this name is very problematic. See
H. Swoboda, *PW* 7 (1912) s.v. "Gobryas," col. 1151, 2 and 4.

[60]The Scholiast identifies them as Apollo and Artemis.

[61]Guthrie (*History*, 5.396) notes that Herodotus (4.33)
refers to "sacred offerings" that will come to Delos from
the mysterious Hyperboreans. He raises, then, a question

concerning pseudo-Plato's source of information for the
bronze tablets, "if indeed the author did not invent it."
Now metals were used as writing materials, and bronze
plaques inscribed with legal texts or dedications are
common (cf. the "Orphic Gold Leaves," G. Zuntz, *Persephone*
[Oxford: Clarendon, 1971] 277ff.).  In a note to Blakeney
(p. 42), H. J. Rose wrote:
> This refers to the Hyperborean maidens, who were
> four (or rather 2 x 2) in number (Herod. IV, 33
> and 35); according to Callimachus three, their
> names being Oupis, Loxos and Hecaerge (*h. ad
> Delum*, 292); two here.  I can remember no other
> passage which gives that number, but the names
> agree with those mentioned by Callimachus, as
> far as they go, ᾽Ωπις and οὖπις being the same.
> I see no reason for supposing them men; the names
> are feminine, ῾Εκάεργος being a blunder of some-
> one who had Apollo's epithet in mind (from which
> indeed the name is formed, as the others are also
> from names or titles of one or other of the di-
> vine twins.

The Hyperboreans were a legendary people belonging to
Apollo (who were sometimes located in the far North or in
the South-East or India); poets such as Pindar (*P*. 10.49-
56) praised their virtue and blessedness.  See also Hdt.
4.32-36 who doubted their existence and Antoninus Liberalis
20 for an interesting connection between Apollo and the
Hyperboreans.  The Pythagoreans loved to relate legends
about the Hyperboreans and called Pythagoras himself "Hy-
perborean Apollo" (see Burkert, *Lore and Science*, 91f.,
149-50 and index).  But there is also mention of Orpheus
receiving an oracle from Apollo Hyperboreus (Servius ad
Vergil *Aen*. III 98, quoted in Kern, *Orphicorum Fragmenta*,
83).  Some of what Gobryas learns from the tablets is
Orphic-Pythagorean.

[62]"Αδηλον is possibly a pun on Hades' name (᾽Αΐδης,
lit. the "Unseen").

[63]The spherical (σφαιροειδῆς) heaven seems to be a
recollection of Plato *Ti*. 33B: the Demiurge fashioned the
universe into "the shape of a sphere (σφαιροειδές), equi-
distant in all directions from the center to the extremi-
ties, which of all shapes is the most perfect and self-
similar."  Nilsson noted that this scientifically conceived
notion of the universe in the *Axiochus* stands in opposition
to the mythological one following (*Geschichte*, 2.241-42).
See also I. Opelt, "Erde," *RAC* 5 (1962) esp. 1150 and 1155
for philosophical notions similar to that found here.

[64]The brothers are probably Zeus, Poseidon, and Hades
among whom the cosmos was divided (see *Il*. 15.187f.); the
children of brothers are probably Minos and Rhadamanthys
(371B) who are always considered sons of Zeus.  The story

of the Olympians casting lots for their positions (cf. ἔλαχον here with the ἔλαχον of *Il.* 15.190f., and esp. 191, παλλομένων, "when lots were cast") is found also in Apollodorus I.2,1.

[65]Two of the "four infernal rivers" mentioned often in antiquity beginning with Homer (e.g. *Od.* 10.513-14: "there (in Hades' dark house) into Acheron flow Periphlege-thon and Cocytus").

[66]Two of the legendary judges of the dead, mentioned together for the first time in Plato, *Grg.* 523E and *Ap.* 41A; see Nilsson, *Geschichte*, 1.821ff.

[67]The "plain of Truth" occurs at *Phdr.* 248B and in the *Hermetica* (ed. Scott, 3.583); cf. the "plain of oblivion" (Λήθης), Plato, *R.* 10.621A and Ar. *Ra.* 186 and Luc. *Luct.* 5.

[68]On the "good *daimon*," see Nilsson, *Geschichte*, 1.218ff. and especially 2.213ff. A distinction between good and bad *daimones* was made by Xenocrates (see R. Heinze, *Xenocrates*, 78ff.; Dillon, *Middle Platonists*, 31ff.; and Guthrie, *History*, 5.475).

[69]The phrase χωρὸς εὐσεβῶν is found on a number of inscriptions sometime after the second century B.C. (see *Epigrammata gr. ex lapid. collecta*, ed. Kaibel, 151,5; 186,9; 218,16; 291; 411,4; 506,8). Cf. εὐσεβῶν λειμῶνας Diod. 1.96,2 (Kern, *Orphicorum Fragmenta*, 293). The notion that there is a place reserved for the pious in the under-world probably became popular as a result of the mystery cults (see Nilsson, *Geschichte*, 1.647ff., esp. 666f.), but the concept of εὐσέβεια was also an important one in hel-lenistic philosophy (see ibid., 2.253f.).

[70]The fountains of pure water are possibly reminiscent of "cool water flowing from the pool of Memory" on the Orphic Gold Leaves (Kern, *Orphicorum Fragmenta*, *Frag.* 32, p. 105, and Zuntz, *Persephone*, 358ff., esp. 370ff., on Egyptian analogies of the cool drink for the dead; cf. Dieterich, *Nekyia*, 95).

[71]This line and the description following until "... the sun's gentle rays" is poetic, and Dieterich (*Nekyia*, 212) sensed remains of dactylic-logaoedic metre. There are parallels with this passage in Plut. *Consol. ad Apoll.* 120C where Pindar (*Frag.* 129) is quoted (see my introduction to the *Axiochus*) and Plutarch *Frag.* 178: "but after this a marvellous light meets the wanderer, and open country and meadow lands welcome him; and in that place there are voices and dancing and the solemn majesty of sacred music and holy visions. And amidst these, he walks at large in

a new freedom, now perfect and fully initiated, celebrating the sacred rites, a garland upon his head, and converses with pure and holy men...." (Sandbach's trans., Plutarch, XV, *LCL* [1969]; on the fragment and its Eleusinian or Orphic ideas, see H. D. Betz, "Fragmenta 21-23, 157-158, 176-178," *Plutarch's Theological Writings and Early Christian Literature* [Leiden, 1975] 321ff.).

[72] Κυκλίοισι χοροῖς appears in the Orphic hymn to the ῞Ωραι (Seasons) (G. Quandt, *Orphei Hymni* [2nd ed.; Berlin: Weidmann, 1962] 43.8, pp. 33-34) where the Moirai and Charites lead Persephone back to the light with "cyclic dances" (lit. circular dances about her or about an altar). The words used in the Hymn to describe the Seasons, εἰαριναί, λειμωνιάδες, πολυάνθεοι...παντόχροοι, are similar to those used in the *Axiochus* to describe the λειμῶνες ποικίλοις ἐαριζομένοι; cf. the ὧραι mentioned shortly before the meadows.

[73] Poetic performances, music, drinking parties, feasts are all part of underworld descriptions common in the Greco-Roman period, e.g. Plu. *De sera num. vind.* 565F. Lucian, *VH* 2.14-16 (cf. 5) where the cups fill of themselves (cf. the "self-furnished feasts"). No doubt the descriptions arose from the mysteries, Dionysiac and Orphic cults; see Dieterich, *Nekyia*, 36ff., 75ff.

[74] The temperate climate of the abode of the blessed goes back at least to Homer; see *Od.* 4.563ff.; cf. *Od.* 6.43 where Olympus is said to be shaken neither by winds nor rain nor snow. See also Dieterich, *Nekyia*, 19f.

[75] The "place of honor" is obviously taken from the mysteries; see D.L. 6.39, where the Athenians encourage Diogenes of Sinope to be initiated into the mysteries, for the initiates have places of honor (προεδρίας) in the next world; see also Plut. *Consol. ad Apoll.* 120B where the εὐσεβεῖς, according to a "story of ancient poets and philosophers," receive a certain privilege and place of honor (προεδρία) when departed. On the seat of honor in the theater enjoyed by the Hierophant of the Eleusinian cult, see Mylonas, *Eleusis*, 230.

[76] This is an important, but puzzling, sentence. First, the expression γεννήτης τῶν θεῶν has caused some discussion. Wilamowitz (*Gött. Gel. Anz.* 1896, p. 984) thought Axiochus was so called only as a member of the *genos* (house or clan) of the Εὐπατρίδαι to which he apparently belonged. To be sure, at Athens it was possible to be adopted into a *genos* and the person was inscribed εἰς τοὺς γεννήτας of the adopter (Is. 7.13, 15, 17, 43; see also the remark of the Scholiast who interprets γεννήτας as

"those arranged into the *genē* [houses] of Athens"). Rohde,
however, maintained that Axiochus is so called because he
shares in the privileges of the initiated (μεμυημένοι). He
is thus akin to the gods because he is initiated (Rohde,
*Psyche*, 602-603).

Mylonas, however, who accepts F. R. Walton's view in
"Kinsman of the Gods?" (*CP* 58 [1953] 24-27), does not
think the line proves a theory of divine adoption of the
initiate, but means only a "worshipper of Demeter." Thus
Axiochus can share in the privileges of those who have been
initiated since he is one of the band of these, the wor-
shippers of Demeter (Mylonas, *Eleusis*, 296 n. 23). This
may be correct, but there nonetheless seems to be a kinship to the divine in that Axiochus has a soul in which a
divine spirit is present (370C).

Secondly, it remains unclear why Axiochus is called
πρῶτος, presumably before other initiates. Nothing in the
text explains this, and all that can be affirmed is that
his divine kinship seems based on his initiation at Eleusis
(see the lines following in the text).

There are similarities to the present notion. For
example, the expression Θεὸς ἐγένου ἐξ ἀνθρώπου appears on
the Orphic Gold Leaves (see Zuntz, *Persephone*, 329ff.); in
the *Somnium Scipionis* (Cic. *Rep.* VI.24-26) Scipio, having
been informed that the mind (*mens*) not the body is the
true self, is told: "Know, then, that you are a god (*deum
te igitur scito esse*) if a god is that which lives, feels,
remembers...which rules, governs and moves the body...just
as the ruler god (*princeps deus*) rules the universe" (see
H. Betz, "The Delphic Maxim," 474f. on this passage).
Like Scipio, Axiochus has come to much the same realization
that a divine spirit is in him (see 370C-D).

[77]The Scholiast identifies the goddess at Eleusis as
Demeter. The tradition that both Heracles and Dionysus
were initiated at Eleusis is represented in vase paintings
(on Heracles' initiation, see also Apollod. 2.5.12, Plu.
*Thes.* 30.5, Diod. 4.14,3; Mylonas, *Eleusis*, 205ff. and
213; and N. J. Richardson, *The Homeric Hymn to Demeter*
[Oxford: Oxford University, 1974] 22f. and 212f.). Moreover, Dionysus was sometimes confused with Iacchos, the
personification of the shoutings and enthusiasm of the
initiates (see Nilsson, *Geschichte*, 1.664, and Mylonas,
*Eleusis*, 307f.). The descents of Dionysos (to bring back
his mother) and of Heracles (to bring up Cerberus, or to
return Alcestis) into the underworld are well known, and
they may well have prepared themselves by being initiated.
Here they are coupled as the two most illustrious initiates
ever initiated.

[78]The function of the Furies or Erinyes to send the
wicked to the place of the impious (Χῶρος ἀσεβῶν) is also
found at Luc. *Luct.* 8. On the Erinyes, see B. D. Dietrich,

*Death, Fate, and the Gods* (London, 1965) 91ff. Originally
they were not spirits of vengeance, but chthonic deities
linked with Demeter (ibid., 117f.). In Orphic belief,
however, they were considered avengers of human guilt,
their parents were Hades and Persephone (ibid., 93f.).
Also the mention of Erebus (the place of darkness and son
of Chaos. Hes. *Th.* 123) together with Chaos and Tartarus
probably reflects Orphic influence (in Ar. *Av.* 690f. =
Kern, *Orphicorum Fragmenta* 1, p. 80, they are mentioned
together); see also Damasc. *De princ.* 123 (Kern, *Orphicorum
Fragmenta* 54) and Nilsson's comments on Erebus in Neo-
pythagoreanism and Orphism (*Geschichte*, 2.426f.).

[79]Lit. "the endless (ἀτελεῖς (possibly also with the
sense of "unitiated") drawings of water of the Danaids."
On this punishment, cf. Hor. *Car.* 3.11,21-24 and see the
most recent study of the Danaids by E. Keuls (*The Water
Carriers in Hades* [Amsterdam, 1974] esp. 53f.) for this
passage.

[80]A *locus classicus* for the punishment of these arch-
sinners of antiquity is *Od.* 11.583ff. They are often
mentioned in later literature, e.g. Lucr. 3.980f.

[81]On the Avengers or Ποιναί, see Dieterich (*Nekyia*,
58-59). Their distinction from the Furies or Erinyes is
not always clear; both are spirits of punishment (cf. Luc.
*Luct.* 6, where they are mentioned together).

[82]These last remarks are reminiscent of Plato, *Phd.*
107D: "But since the soul is seen to be immortal, it cannot escape from evil or be saved in any other way than by
becoming as good and wise as possible. For the soul takes
with it to Hades nothing but its education and nurture,
and these are said to benefit or injure the departed greatly from the very beginning of its journey there." Cf. the
proof for the soul's immortality at *Phdr.* 245C beginning
ψυχὴ πᾶσα ἀθάνατος. Belief in the soul's immortality was
according to the second century philosopher Atticus (Eusebius, *PE* 15.809) the cement which holds together the Platonic School; without it, Plato's whole philosophy collapses.

[83]Cf. Plato, *Phd.* 67Dff. where it is claimed that the
philosopher, because he truly loves wisdom, desires the
separation of the soul from the body, or death. On the
notion that death is not an evil, possibly in connection
with the mysteries, cf. the grave inscription cited by W.
Peek (*Griechische Vers-Inschriften* [Berlin, 1955] no. 879,
p. 242): "...he went to the immortals; indeed lovely is the
secret revealed by the blessed, that death is not an evil
for mortals, but a good" (ἢ καλὸν ἐκ μακάρων μυστήριον, οὐ
μόνον εἶναι τὸν θάνατον θνητοῖς οὐ κακὸν ἀλλ' ἀγαθόν). See
also Burkert, *Griechische Religion*, 431. Finally, compare
Socrates' closing remark with 366 B above.

# SELECT BIBLIOGRAPHY

Arrighetti, G. *Epicuro: Opere* (= *Classici della Filo-sofia*, IV). Turin: G. Einaudi, 1960.

Betz, H. D. "The Delphic Maxim ΓΝΩΘΙ ΣΑΥΤΟΝ in Hermetic Interpretation." *Harvard Theological Review* 63 (1970) 465-484.

Blakeney, E. H. *The Axiochus: On Death and Immortality*. London: F. Muller, 1937.

Brinkmann, A. "Beiträge zur Kritik und Erklärung des Dialogs *Axiochos*." *Rheinisches Museum* 51 (1896) 441-454.

Buresch, C. *Consolationum a Graecis Romanisque scriptarum historia critica* (= *Leipziger Studien zur Klassischen Philologie*, IX/1). Leipzig: S. Hirzel, 1886.

Burkert, W. *Lore and Science in Ancient Pythagoreanism*. Trans. E. L. Minar, Jr. Cambridge, MA: Harvard, 1972.

_____. *Griechische Religion der archaischen und klassischen Epoche* (= *Die Religionen der Menschheit*, XV). Stuttgart: Kohlhammer, 1977.

Chevalier, J. *Etude critique du dialogue pseudo-platonicien l'Axiochos*. Paris: F. Alcan, 1915.

Corsson, P. "Cicero's Quelle für *Tusc. I.*" *Rheinisches Museum* 36 (1881) 506-523.

Courcelle, P. O. *'Consolation de Philosophie' dans la tradition littéraire. Antécédents et postérité de Boèce*. Paris: Etudes Augustiniennes, 1967.

Dieterich, A. *Nekyia*. Leipzig, 1893; 3rd ed., Stuttgart: B. G. Teubner, 1969.

Dillon, J. *The Middle Platonists*. London: G. Duckworth, 1977.

Feddersen, H. *Über den pseudoplatonischen Dialog Axiochus*. Programm Cuxhaven: G. Rauschenplat, 1895.

Festugière, A. J. *Epicurus and his Gods*. Cambridge, MA: Harvard, 1956.

Guthrie, W. K. C. *Orpheus and Greek Religion*. 2nd ed. London: Methuen, 1952.

_____. *The Greeks and their Gods*. Boston: Beacon, 1954 (reprint).

Guthrie, W. K. C. *A History of Greek Philosophy*, I-V.
    Cambridge, England: Cambridge University, 1962-1978.

Hani, J. *Plutarque. Consolation à Apollonios* (= *Etudes et
    Commentaires*, LXXVIII). Paris: Klincksieck, 1972.

Heidel, W. A. *Pseudo-Platonica*. Baltimore, 1896; reprint,
    New York: Arno, 1976.

Heinze, R. *Xenokrates*. Leipzig: Teubner, 1892.

Hermann, C. F. *Platonis Dialogi*, VI. Leipzig: B. G.
    Teubner, 1907.

Immisch, O. *Philologische Studien zu Plato*, I: *Axiochus*.
    Leipzig: B. G. Teubner, 1896.

Judeich, W. *Topographie von Athen*. 2nd ed., *Handbuch der
    Altertumswissenschaft* III.2.2. Munich: Beck, 1931.

Kern, O. *Orphicorum Fragmenta*. Berlin: Weidmann, 1922;
    reprinted, 1963.

Meister, M. *De "Axiocho" dialogo*. Breslau: W. G. Korn,
    1915.

Mylonas, G. E. *Eleusis and the Eleusinian Mysteries*.
    Princeton: Princeton University, 1961.

Nilsson, M. P. *Geschichte der griechischen Religion*, II:
    *Die hellenistische und römische Zeit*. 2nd ed., *Hand-
    buch der Altertumswissenschaft* V.2.2. Munich: Beck,
    1961.

O'Neil, E. N. *Teles (The Cynic Teacher)*. Missoula:
    Scholars Press, 1977.

Padelford, F. M. *The Axiochus of Plato Translated by
    Edmund Spenser*. Baltimore: Johns Hopkins, 1934.

Quandt, G. *Orphei Hymni*. 2nd ed. Berlin: Weidmann, 1962.

Richardson, N. J. *The Homeric Hymn to Demeter*. Oxford:
    Oxford University, 1974.

Rist, J. *Epicurus: An Introduction*. Cambridge, England:
    Cambridge University, 1972.

Rohde, E. *Psyche*. Trans. W. B. Hillis. London: Routledge,
    & Kegan Paul, 1950 (reprint).

Shorey, P. *What Plato Said*. Chicago: University of
    Chicago, 1968 (reprint).

Souilhé, J.  *Platon: Oeuvres Complètes*, XIII, Part 3.
    Paris: Budé, 1930.

Tarán, L.  *Academica: Plato, Philip of Opus, and the
    Pseudo-Platonic Epinomis*.  Philadelphia: American
    Philosophical Society, 1975.

Taylor, A. E.  *Plato: The Man and his Work*.  New York:
    Meridian, 1956 (reprint).

Wyncherley, R.  *The Stones of Athens*.  Princeton: Prince-
    ton University, 1978.

Zuntz, G.  *Persephone*.  Oxford: Oxford University, 1971.

## NAMES, ANCIENT AND MODERN

Academus, 60 (n. 32)
Academy, 11, 19, 21, 35, 53 (n. 1), 60 (n. 32)
Acheron, 47, 67 (n. 65)
Acropolis, 60 (n. 33)
Aelian, 12
Aeschines, 10-11
Agamedes, 20, 37, 61 (nn. 38, 39)
Alcestis, 69 (n. 77)
Alcibiades, 53 (n. 2), 63 (n. 50)
Alexandrian Platonists, 18
Amphiaraus, 39, 61 (n. 41)
Amazon column, 31, 53 (n. 1)
Antiope, 53 (n. 1)
Antisthenes, 53 (n. 1)
Apollo, 39, cf. 47
    Apollo Hyperboreus, 65 (n. 60), 66 (n. 61)
    Apollo Lyceius, 60 (n. 32)
Areopagus and Council of, 13, 25 (n. 25), 37, 60 (n. 33),
        62 (n. 47)
Arginusae, 13, 63 (n. 48)
Argine priestess (i.e. Cydippe), 20, 37, 61 (n. 39)
Aristides Rhetor, 12
Ariston of Chios, 53 (n. 1)
Aristotle, 11, 60 (n. 32)
Artemis, 47, 65 (n. 60)
Athena Itonia, 53 (n. 1)
Athens, Athenian(s), 1, 5, 13, 29, 35, 53 (nn. 1-2),
        56 (n. 15), 59 (nn. 26, 29), 60 (nn. 31, 33),
        62 (n. 47), 63 (n. 49), 68 (nn. 75, 76), 69 (n. 76)
Attic, 11, 55 (n. 9)
Atticus, 70 (n. 82)
Avengers, 49, 70 (n. 81)
Axiochus, 8-10, 17, 21, 23 (n. 5), 29, 31, 33, 35, 41, 43,
        45, 49, 53 (n. 2), 55 (nn. 7, 8, 10), 62 (n. 45),
        63 (n. 54), 65 (n. 58), 68 (n. 76), 69 (n. 76)
*Axiochus*, 1-21, 23 (nn. 1-5), 53 (n. 1), 54 (nn. 3-4),
        57 (n. 16), 58 (n. 24), 59 (nn. 25, 28, 29), 61 (nn.
        37, 39), 63 (nn. 51, 52), 66 (n. 63), 68 (n. 72)

Bias, 39, 62 (n. 44)
Bion of Borysthenes, 16, 17, 62 (n. 44)
Biton, 61 (n. 39), cf. 37

Callias, 35, 59 (n. 26)
Callirrhoe, 13, 29, 53 (n. 1)
Callixenus, 41, 63 (nn. 49, 50)
Centaur, 43, 63 (n. 52); see Cheiron

Cerberus, 69 (n. 77)
Chaos, 49, 70 (n. 78)
Charites, 68 (n. 72)
Charmides, 8, 29, 53 (n. 2)
Cheiron, 63 (n. 52); see Centaur
Christian, Christianity, 1, 5-7, 21
Cicero, 3, 18
Cleinias, 8, 9, 29, 53 (nn. 1-2), 54 (n. 5)
Cleisthenes, 33, 56 (n. 15)
Clement of Alexandria, 12
Cleobis, 61 (n. 39), cf. 37
Cocytus, 47, 67 (n. 65)
Crantor, 19-20, 23, 61 (n. 42)
Crates, 16
Cratinus, 60 (n. 36)
Critias, 53 (n. 2)
Critobulus, 53 (n. 2)
Cydippe, 61 (n. 39); see Argive priestess
Cynic, Cynicism, 1, 8, 16, 18, 20, 22, 53 (n. 1), 55 (n. 6),
    59 (n. 24), 62 (n. 44)
Cynosarges, 13, 29, 49, 53 (n. 1)


Damon, 8, 29, 54 (n. 2)
Danaids, 49, 70 (n. 79)
Delos, 9, 47
Demeter, 4, cf. 49, 69 (nn. 76, 77), 70 (n. 78)
Diogenes Laertius, 5, 11
Diogenes of Sinope, 5, 68 (n. 75)
Diomeian gates, 53 (n. 1)
Dionysiac cults, 68 (n. 73)
Dionysus, 4, 5, 24 (n. 11), 49, 69 (n. 77)
Draco, 33, 56 (n. 15)


Egyptian, 67 (n. 70)
Eleusis, Eleusinian, 4, 5, 24 (n. 11), 49, 68 (nn. 71, 75),
    69 (nn. 76, 77)
Elysian plain, 3
Enneacrounos, 53 (n. 1)
Ephebes, 13, 15, 25 (n. 25), 35, 37, 60 (n. 31)
Ephialtes, 41, 62 (n. 47)
Epicharmus, 35, 59 (n. 25)
Epicurus, Epicurean(s), Epicureanism, 1, 2, 8, 10, 11,
    14-16, 18, 20, 21, 23 (n. 5), 25 (n. 32), 56 (n. 14),
    57 (nn. 16, 19), 63 (n. 53)
Erebus, 49, 70 (n. 78)
Erinyes, 69-70 (n. 78), 70 (n. 81); see Furies
Eumolpus, 24 (n. 10)
Euryptolemus, 41, 63 (n. 50)


Furies, 49, 70 (n. 81); see Erinyes

Galen, 12
Garden, 21
Glaucon, 29
Gobyras, 9, 47, 49, 65 (n. 59), 66 (n. 61)
Gymnasium, 35


Hades, 4, 49, 66 (nn. 62, 64), 67 (n. 65), 70 (n. 78)
Hecademus, 60 (n. 32)
Hecaerge, 47, 66 (n. 61)
Hera, 37
Heracles, 4, 5, 24 (n. 11), 49, 53 (n. 1), 58 (n. 24),
      69 (n. 27)
Hilarion (Theodorus Prodromus), 6
Hippocles, 19
Hipponichus, 32
Homer, 5
Hyperboreans, 47, 65-66 (n. 61)


Iacchos, 69 (n. 77)
Ilisus, 13, 29, 53 (n. 1)
Itonian gates, 31, 53 (n. 1)


Loxos, 66 (n. 61)
Lucian, 12
Lyceum, 35, 53 (n. 1), 60 (n. 32)


Middle Platonism, 18, 20
Miltiades, 41, 62 (n. 47)
Minos, 1, 47, 66 (n. 64), 67 (n. 66)
Moirai, 68 (n. 72)
Mormo, 54 (n. 5)


Odeion, 53 (n. 1)
Olympeion, 53 (n. 1)
Olympus, 68 (n. 74)
Opis (Oupis), 47, 66 (n. 61)
Orpheus, Orphic(s), Orphism, 1, 2, 4, 5, 23 (n. 6), 24
      (nn. 6, 7), 56 (n. 11), 57 (n. 17), 66 (n. 61),
      68 (nn. 71-73), 69 (n. 76), 70 (nn. 78, 79)
Oupis; see Opis


Paul, the apostle, 6
Pericles, 54 (n. 2), 62 (n. 47)
Peripatetics, 18
Periphlegethon, 67 (n. 68)
Persephone, 68 (n. 72), 70 (n. 78)
Phalerum, 53 (n. 1)
Philo of Alexandria, 18
Philodemus, 12
Pindar, 5
Plain of Truth, 47

Plato, Platonic, i, 1, 2, 5, 8, 10-16, 18, 20-21, 23 (n.
    5), 24 (n. 7), 53 (n. 2), 57 (nn. 16-17), 58 (nn.
    21, 24), 59 (nn. 24, 28), 60 (n. 32), 66 (n. 61),
    70 (n. 82)
Pleiades, 45, 64 (n. 56)
Plutarch, 3, 11, 13
Pluto, 47
Polybius, 12
Poseidon, 66 (n. 64)
Poseidonius, 3, 11, 18
Potideia, 57 (n. 20)
Prodicus, of Ceos, 9, 13, 35, 41, 58 (n. 24), 63 (n. 51)
Pythagoras, Pythagorianism, 1, 2, 5, 11, 23-24 (n. 6),
    66 (n. 61)
Pytho, 37

Rhadamanthys, 1, 47, 66 (n. 64), 67 (n. 66)
Roman, 13, 57 (n. 20)

Scipio, 69 (n. 76)
Scylla, 43
Semele, cf. 69 (n. 77)
Seneca, 3, 18
Septuagint (LXX), 6
Sextus Empiricus, 15
Sisyphus, 4, 49
Socrates, 1, 3, 8-10, 13-15, 17, 19, 23 (n. 5), 29-51
    passim, 53 (n. 1), 54 (n. 3), 55 (n. 10), 57 (n. 16),
    58 (nn. 21-24), 59 (n. 27), 62 (n. 45), 63 (nn. 48,
    51, 53, 54), 64 (n. 57), 70 (n. 83)
Sophist(s), 55 (n. 24), 59 (n. 26)
Stilpon, 56 (n. 13)
Stobaeus, 62 (nn. 42, 46)
Stoic(s), Stoicism, 1, 6, 8, 10, 16-18, 20, 24 (n. 9),
    53 (n. 1), 55 (n. 6), 57 (n. 20), 65 (n. 58)

Tantalus, 4, 49
Tartarus, 49, 70 (n. 78)
Teles, 16-17, 59 (n. 28), 61 (n. 36)
Themistocles, 41, 62 (n. 47)
Theodorus Prodomus; see Hilarion
Therames, 41, 63 (n. 49)
Theophrastus, 19
Thrasybulus, 53 (n. 2)
Tityus, 4, 49
Trophonius, 20, 37, 61 (nn. 38, 39)

Xenocrates, i, 6, 11, 16, 19, 23 (n. 3), 25 (n. 31),
    67 (n. 68)
Xerxes, 47, 65 (n. 59)

Zeus, 39, 61 (n. 41), 66 (n. 64)

ANCIENT PASSAGES

Achilles Tatius
  II.36,3   5

Aelian
  *VH* 90.29   12

Aesop
  *Fab*. 84   56 (n. 12)

Andocides
  I.16   53 (n. 2)

Antoninus Liberalis
  20   66 (n. 61)

Apollodorus
  1.2,1   67 (n. 64)
  2.5,12   69 (n. 77)

Appian
  *BC* 2.67   12
     5.125   12

Aristides Rhetor
  *Or*. XII.136   12

Aristophanes
  *Av*. 690f.   70 (n. 78)
  *Nu*. 266   58 (n. 22)
       1417   61 (n. 36)
  *Ra*. 186   67 (n. 67)

Aristotle
  *Ath. Pol*. 42   13
  *Pol*. 1336a 41ff.   59 (n. 29)

Athenaeus
  V.196A   12
  XII.538C   12
  XIII.579A   12
       604E   12

Callimachus
  *h. ad Del*. 292   66 (n. 61)

Cicero
  *Acad*. II.44,135   19-20

Cicero
  *Divin.* I.40    55 (n. 7)
  *Rep.* VI.24-26   69 (n. 76)
  *Tusc.*         19
    I.25,63     64 (n. 57)
    37-38      20
    38,91      56 (n. 14)
    39,93      60 (n. 35)
    47,113-114  20, 61 (n. 38)
    48,115     61 (n. 42)

Clement of Alexandria
  *Strom.* V.94,3   57 (n. 18)

*Collection of Ancient Greek Inscriptions in the British Museum*
  IV.2 (1916) 1062   24 (n. 9)

*Corpus Hermeticum*
  Frag. 25.4   67 (n. 67)
      V       57 (n. 18)
  XIII.12,15   5

*Corpus Inscriptionum Atticarum*
  I.442   57 (n. 20)

*Corpus Inscriptionum Latinarum*
  IX.4840   56 (n. 14)

Crantor
  *Consolatio*   19-21, 61 (n. 42)

Damascius
  *De Princ.* 123   70 (n. 78)

Democritus
  B37   5
  B187  5

Dio Chrysostom
  19(36),42   65 (n. 58)

Diodorus Siculus
  1.96,2   67 (n. 69)
  4.14,3   69 (n. 77)
  20.51   56 (n. 12)

Diogenes Laertius
  2.61   10, cf. 11
  3.62   10
  4.12   11, 19
  5.44   19
  6.1,13   53 (n. 1)

Diogenes Laertius
    6.39          5, 68 (n. 75)
   10.81          56 (n. 14)
     124-129      56 (n. 14)
     139,2        14

Diogenianus Epicureus
    3.25    56 (n. 14)

Diognetus
    6:8    5
    7:2    65 (n. 58)


Epicurus
    *Sent.* 2          2, 14
    *Sent. Vat.* 63    56 (n. 14)

*Epigrammata gr. ex lapid. coll.*
    151,5      67 (n. 69)
    186,9      67 (n. 69)
    218,16     67 (n. 69)
    291        67 (n. 69)
    411,4      67 (n. 69)
    506,8      67 (n. 69)

Euripides
    *Cresph.* Frag. 452 (Dind.)    61 (n. 42)
    *El.* 59                       57 (n. 20)
    *Hel.* 1014-1016              57 (n. 20)

Eusebius
    *PE* 15.809    70 (n. 82)

Herodotus
    1.31       61 (n. 39)
    4.32-36    65-66 (n. 61)
    7.72       65 (n. 58)

Hesiod
    *Th.* 123    70 (n. 78)

Homer
    *Il.* 15.187f.       66 (n. 64)
         15.190-191      67 (n. 64)
         17.446-447      61 (n. 40)
         24.525-526      61 (n. 40)
    *Od.*  4.563-569     3, 68 (n. 74)
          6.43           68 (n. 74)
         10.513-514      67 (n. 65)
         11.575-600      4
             583ff.      70 (n. 80)
         15.187-188      66 (n. 64)
             245-246     61 (n. 41)

*Homeric Hymn to Demeter*
  22-23        69 (n. 77)
  212-213      69 (n. 77)
  480-482      4-5

Horace
  *Car.* 3.11,21-24    70 (n. 79)

Iamblichus
  *Vita Pyth.* 58    56 (n. 12)

Isaeus
  7,13,15,17,43      68 (n. 76)

Ioscrates
  *Paneg.* 28    5

John Chrysostom
  7.408    56 (n. 12)

Lucian
  *Dial. Mort.* 27.9    55 (n. 6)
  *Herm.* 6              55 (n. 6)
  *Luct.* 5             67 (n. 67)
          6             70 (n. 81)
          8             69 (n. 78)
  *Par.* 32            11
  *VH* 2.5              4
      2.14             4
      2.14-16          68 (n. 73)

Lucretius
  3.830-831    56 (n. 14)
    980-981    70 (n. 80)

Marcus Aurelius
  2.17    56 (n. 11)
  7.47    65 (n. 58)

Menander
  *Dysk.* 604-605    62 (n. 45)
  Frag. 125          61 (nn. 37, 41)

*Novum Testamentum*
  Acts 17:19    60 (n. 33)
  2 Cor 5:4     5
       5:17     5
  Eph 4:24      5

*Novum Testamentum*
  Gal 6:15          5
  Heb  4:12         6
       11:13        56 (n. 11)
  1 Pet 1:1         56 (n. 11)
        2:11        56 (n. 11)
  2 Pet 1:13-14     5
  Rom 7:6           5
      8:16          6
  1 Thess 5:23      6


*Orphic Hymn ad Horas*
  (43).8     68 (n. 72)

*Orphicorum Fragmenta* (Kern)
    1     70 (n. 78)
   32     67 (n. 70)
   83     66 (n. 61)
  293     67 (n. 69)


*Papyri Graecae Magicae*     5
    I.319        57 (n. 18)
   IV.448        57 (n. 18)
      1951       57 (n. 18)
      1970       57 (n. 18)
      2141       57 (n. 18)
  XII.251        65 (n. 58)
  XIII.575       65 (n. 58)

Petronius
  *Sat.* 45     59 (n. 25)

Philo Jud.
  *Quaest. in Gen* 1.28              57 (n. 18)
  *Quod det. pot. insid.* 87-90   64 (n. 57)

Philodemus
  *Ira* p. 33 (Wilke)     56 (n. 14)
  *Mort.* 38              60 (n. 34)

Philostratus
  *VS* 38.21     12

Pindar
  *O.*  9.52          62 (n. 43)
  *P.* 10.49-56       66 (n. 61)
  Frag. 2            61 (n. 38)
       129-130       3-4, 67 (n. 71)

Plato
```
Alcb. I.130        57 (n. 16)
Ap.  18B           58 (n. 22)
     32A-C         63 (n. 48)
     40C           19
     40C-D         58 (n. 21)
     40E           14
     41A           67 (n. 66)
Chm. 154           53 (n. 2)
     155A          53 (n. 2)
Cra. 384B          58 (n. 24)
     400C          57 (n. 17)
Epin.              57 (n. 20)
    973D-974D      59 (n. 28)
    974A           61 (n. 36)
    983B           64 (n. 57)
Euthyphr. 271B     53 (n. 2)
          273A     53 (n. 2)
          274B     53 (n. 2)
          275A     53 (n. 2)
Grg.               1
    493A           1, 57 (n. 17)
    523E           67 (n. 66)
Hp. Ma.
    282B           58 (n. 23)
Lg.  646A          60 (n. 36)
     764A          64 (n. 55)
     794C          59 (n. 29)
Ly.  203A          53 (n. 1)
Phd.               1
     62B           1, 57 (n. 17)
     66B           15
     67D           70 (n. 83)
     81C           57 (n. 18)
     82E           57 (n. 17)
     82F           1
     106C          64 (n. 55)
     107D          70 (n. 82)
     114B-C        1
Phdr. 245C         14, 70 (n. 82)
      246B         15, 67 (n. 67)
Prt.               59 (n. 26)
    315A           53 (n. 2)
R.   10            1
     363C          4
     611B          15
     616B-C        57 (n. 20)
     621A          67 (n. 67)
Smp. 172A          53 (n. 1)
     222B          53 (n. 2)
Thg. 128D          53 (n. 2)
Ti.                57 (n. 20)
    32C            15
    33B            66 (n. 63)
```

Plutarch
  *Cons. ad Apoll.*               19
    107A                          55 (n. 6)
    108E-F                        20
    108F                          61 (n. 39)
    109A                          20
    109A-B                        61 (n. 38)
    109F                          20
    119E                          61 (n. 37)
    120B                          68 (n. 75)
    120C                          3-4, 20, 67 (n. 71)
  *De def. or.* 432D              24 (n. 9)
  *De gen. Socr.* 590-592F        3
  *De sera num. vind.* 563B-568   3
  *De sollert. anim.* 963B        12
  *Paral. Graec.* 305D            55 (n. 6)
  Frag. 178                       67 (n. 71)
  *CM* 1                          5
  *CG* 17                         12
  *Cic.* 24                       60 (n. 33)
  *Eum.* 1                        12
  *Num.* 4,6                      24 (n. 9)
  *Thes.* 30.5                    69 (n. 77)
  *Tim.* 38                       12

Polybius
  4.4,2    12
  32.4,5   12

Seneca
  *Apocol.* 9              59 (n. 25)
  *Cons. Helv.* 20         64 (n. 57)
  *Cons. Polyb.* 29        17
  *Epist. Mor.* 66.12      24 (n. 9)

Septuagint (LXX)      5
  Gen 23:4            56 (n. 11)
  Ps 39:12            56 (n. 11)

Servius
  *ad Aen.* III.98    66 (n. 61)

Sextus Empiricus
  *M.* 1.285    14
  *P.* 3.229    14

Sophocles
  *El.* 276    54 (n. 5)

Stobaeus
  98,75 (Mein.) III.236      6
  120,34-35 (Mein.) IV.121   6
  121,38 (Mein.) IV.121      6

Tacitus
  *Ann.* 15.62    17

Teles (O'Neil)
    I.17ff. (3-4H)          56 (n. 13)
   II.149ff. (15-16H)      17, 59 (n. 28)
  III.9-36 (22-23H)        56 (n. 13)
    V.1ff. (49-51H)        16-17, 59 (n. 28)
      32-33 (50H)          61 (n. 36)

Theocritus
  15.40     54 (n. 5)


Xenophon
  *HG* 1.7,12-15      63 (n. 48)
     2.4,19           53 (n. 2)
  *Mem.* 1.1,10       58 (n. 23)
       1.1,18         63 (n. 48)
       1.3,8          53 (n. 2)
       1.3,10         53 (n. 2)
       2.1,21-34      58 (n. 24)
       3.7            53 (n. 2)
       4.4,2          63 (n. 48)
  *Smp.*              59 (n. 26)
     4.12ff.          53 (n. 2)

ἀγαθά (τά)            56 (n. 13)
ἀγαθὸς δαίμων         16
ἄδηλον               66 (n. 62)
Ἀΐδης                66 (n. 62)
αἰθήρ                18, 32, 57 (n. 20)
αἰφνίδιος            12, 54 (n. 4)
ἀμέμπτως             55 (n. 6)
ἀμυχαῖος             12
ἀναισθησία           56 (n. 14)
ἀνασφῆλαι            12
ἀνεπιστασία          56 (n. 14)
ἀνεπιλογίστως        56 (n. 14)
ἄνθρωπος             15, 57 (n. 16)
ἀπηχήματα            12
ἀποδέδεικται         14
ἀστενακτί            12, 55 (n. 6)
ἀτελεῖς              70 (n. 79)
ἀτυχήσεις μου        12
αὐτοχορήγητος        12
ἀφή, ἀφάς            12, 55 (n. 8)
ἀψίκορος             12

βάναυσος             62 (n. 43)

γέγονα καινός        5
γεννήτης (τῶν θεῶν)  68-69 (n. 76)
γνῶμαι               59 (n. 24)
γραμματικός          60 (n. 30)
γραμματισταί         59 (n. 29)

δαίμων, δαίμονες     16, 57 (n. 20), 67 (n. 68)
δῆλον                62 (n. 45)

διαχλευάζω                      12
δίειμι                          65 (n. 58)
δίμοιρον                        12
δρόμος                          65 (n. 58)
δυσαλθές                        60 (n. 34)
δυσαποσπάστως ἔχειν             56 (n. 12)


ἐγγράφεσθαι εἰς ἐφήβους         13
εἰμαρμένη                       17
ἐκφοβεῖν                        54 (n. 5)
ἐλεούμενον                      62 (n. 46)
ἐπίδειξις                       58 (n. 24)
ἐπίκηρον                        60 (n. 34)
ἐπιτωθάζω                       12
ἐς τὸ χρεὼν ἴη                  12, 17, cf. 55 (n. 6)
εὐδαίμων                        16
εὐσέβεια, εὐσεβεῖν              55 (n. 7), 67 (n. 69), 68 (n. 75)


καινός, καινότης                5
κακοδαίμων                      16
κοινά (τά)                      58 (n. 23)
κοσμητής                        60 (n. 31)
κριτικός                        12, 60 (n. 30)
κροτέω                          55 (n. 9), 62 (n. 46)
κρότησις                        55 (n. 9)
κυκλίοισι χοροῖς                68 (n. 72)


λειμῶνες                        68 (n. 72)
λεσχηνεία                       63 (n. 53)
λόγος                           55 (n. 10)


μάγος                           65 (n. 59)
μεταβολή                        58 (n. 21)
μετεωρολογεῖν                   65 (n. 58)
μετοίκησις                      58 (n. 21)
μίαν αἴσθησιν                   64 (n. 54)
μορμολύττομαι                   54 (n. 5)

νοῦς 16

ὁμοίωσις θεῷ 18, 26 (n. 34)

παιδαγωγός 59 (n. 29)
παιδοτρίβης 13, 59 (n. 29)
πάλαι, καί 65 (n. 58)
παρεπιδημία 12, 56 (n. 11)
παρηγορεῖν 12
περιττά (τά) 58 (n. 23)
περιψυγμός 12
πληθύς 12
πνεῦμα 6, 9, 15, 18, 24 (n. 9)
Ποιναί 70 (n. 81)
ποππύζειν 62 (n. 46)
πόρος 17, 57 (n. 19)
πρᾴως 54 (n. 5)
προεδρία 68 (n. 75)
πρός + gen. 54 (n. 3)
πρὸς κακοῦ 12, 54 (n. 3)
πρῶτος 69 (n. 76)

ῥωμαλέος 12

σῆμα 1, 23 (n. 6)
σκῆνος, σκήνωμα 5-6, 57 (n. 18)
σύγκρισις 15
συνερανίζω 12
σύστασις 15
σφαιροειδές 66 (n. 63)
σῶμα 1, 23 (n. 6)

τακτικός 60 (n. 30)
τέχνη 62 (n. 43)
τοσοῦτος 58 (n. 23)

φευκτός            63 (n. 51)
φλυαρολογία        21
φροντιστής         58 (n. 22)
φύσις              17


χειρωνατικός       62 (n. 43)
χρεία              58-59 (n. 24)
χρεών (τό)         12, 17, 55 (n. 6)
χωρὸς εὐσεβῶν      67 (n. 69), 69 (n. 78)


ψυχή               6, 15, 16, 57 (n. 16)


ὥρα                54 (n. 4)
ὡρακία             54 (n. 4)